Basic Maths for Adults

Everyday Maths Made Simple

By Vali Nasser

ISBN-13: 978-1503052826

ISBN-10: 1503052826

Table of Contents

Introduction

This book is aimed at helping you do every day maths with ease. In addition, if you are applying for jobs that require basic numeracy skills then this book will also be valuable. This will be particularly true if you want to improve your speed in Mental Arithmetic and re-visit some areas in arithmetic, especially if you did your maths a long time ago or do not feel very confident in maths.

Although it is sensible to use calculators for complicated calculations it is important that you can do simple sums with confidence and ease. In addition I am sure you will want to be reminded about how to work out fractions, decimals, percentages, ratios and proportions. Everyday problems often involve being able to estimate as well as being able to work with simple formulas like Speed, Distance and Time and of course, conversions from one type of currency to another when you go on holiday! Finally, basic Statistics is useful to make sense of data that is presented visually or numerically in newspaper articles. All these topics are included in this book.

The last two chapters introduce you to basic algebra and geometry in case you want to progress further in maths.

Just for your information, research has shown that numerical aptitude correlates well with performance and job prospects. Although a lot of the material in the first two chapters may be familiar to you, hopefully you will find some of the 'Speed Methods' introduced helpful for working out basic questions in arithmetic quickly. This will help you to approach basic arithmetical problems with more confidence.

One thing to remember is that there is often more than one way of working out a given problem. It does not matter which method you use, so long as you feel comfortable with it.

About the Author

The author of this book has experience in both consultancy work and teaching.

The author's initial book 'Speed Mathematics Using the Vedic System' has a significant following and has been translated into Japanese and Chinese as well as German. In addition, his book 'Pass the QTS Numeracy Test with ease' is very popular with teacher trainees. Besides being a specialist mathematics teacher the author also has a degree in psychology. This has enabled him to work as an organizational development consultant giving him exposure to psychometric testing particularly applicable to numerical reasoning. Besides working in consultancy he also managed the QTS numeracy tests for teacher trainees at OCR in conjunction with the teaching agency. Subsequently he has tutored and taught mathematics and statistics in schools as well as in adult education.

He hopes that this book 'Basic Maths for Adults' will help those aspiring to pass basic numeracy tests or just brush up their everyday skills.

Chapter 1   Arithmetic part I

Addition and Subtraction using Speed Methods

The normal approach of column addition and subtraction is a good method and if you feel happy with it then you should have no problems with this part of arithmetic. Make sure that when dealing with adding and subtracting decimal numbers, the decimal points are aligned.

Consider the **Speed Method** below for addition

Compensating or adjusting method

In this method we simply adjust by adding or subtracting from the rounded up or rounded down number as shown in the examples below. In example1 we round up 96 to 100 and adjust by taking away 4. Similarly we round up 69 to 70 and adjust by taking away 1. See below for all the working out.

Example1:

$96 + 69 =$

$100 - 4 + 70 - 1 =$

$170 - 5 = 165$

Example2:

$59 + 88 + 23 =$

$60 - 1 + 90 - 2 + 20 + 3$

$150 + 20 - 3 + 3 = 170$

Basic Arithmetic Question

A customer buys three items from a shoe shop, items A, B and C. The selling prices are as follows: A sells for £23.90, B sells for £33.75 and C sells for £19.95. Find the total amount the customer has to pay.

Method:

Total cost = £23.90 + £33.75 + £19.95

= £24 - 10p + £34 - 25p + £20 – 5p = £24 + £34 + £20 - 10p - 25p - 5p

= £78 – 40p = £77.60

Subtraction

You probably remember column subtraction and the number line method from your 'O' level or GCSE days. Before we go on to use the *'Speed Method'* let us revisit the familiar method for subtraction.

Example1:

Work out: 241 - 28

Traditional column method

The traditional methods of subtraction serve us well in mathematics. However, there is one more strategy that we can use to make this process much easier but more of this later. First we will consider the normal approach.

Consider the following example:

$$
\begin{array}{r}
241 \\
- \quad 28 \\
\hline
213 \\
\end{array}
$$

Starting from the right hand side we cannot subtract 8 from 1 so we borrow 1 from the tens column to make the units column 11. Subtracting 8 from 11 gives us 3, however since we have taken away 1 from the tens column we are left with 3 in this column. Subtracting 2 from 3 in the tens column gives us 1. Since we have nothing else to take away the final answer is 213.

Speed Method of Subtraction

Example1: Now consider the same problem using a *Speed Method*.

If we add 2 to the top and bottom number we get:

$$
\begin{array}{rl}
243 & (241+2) \\
- \quad 30 & (28+2) \\
\hline
213 & \\
\end{array}
$$

You can see that subtracting 30 from 243 is easier than subtracting 28 from 241!

This strategy relies on the algebraic fact that if you add or subtract the same number from the top and bottom numbers you do not change the answer to the subtraction sum.

So essentially we try and add or subtract a certain number to both the numbers in order to make the sum simpler. A few more examples will help.

Example 2:

```
    113
  -   6
```

Add 4 to both numbers (we want to try to make the units column 0 in the bottom row if we can and if it helps) So the new sum is:

```
    117
  - 10
    107
```

We can see that if we subtract 10 from 117 we get 107.

Example 3:

```
    321
  - 114
```

Let us add 6 to each number so that the unit column in the bottom number becomes a 0 as shown below:

327 (add 6 to 321)

- 120 (add 6 to 114)

207

Subtracting 120 from 327 we get 207 as shown. No borrowing is required.

Note: Sometimes you might find the method above useful; at other times it is easier to revert to the traditional method.

Subtracting from 100, 1000, 10000, 100000

Some people find subtracting from 1000, 10000 or 100000 difficult, so let us consider a useful technique for doing this.

Subtracting from 100, 1000 or 10000 using a *'Speed Method'*

In this case we use the rule **'all from nine and the last from 10'**

Example 1: 100 – 76

We simply take each figure (except the last) in 76 from 9 and the last from 10 as shown below:

$$1\ 0\ 0$$

$$-\ \ 76$$

$$\underline{\qquad 24}$$

Take 7 from 9 to give 2 and take 6 from 10 to give 4

Example 2: 1000 – 897 = 103

We simply take each figure (except the last) in 897 from 9 and the last from 10 as shown below:

$$1\ 0\ 0\ 0$$

$$-8\ 9\ 7$$

$$\underline{\ 1\ 0\ 3}$$

(Take 8 from 9 to give 1. Take 9 from 9 to give 0 and take 7 from 10 to give 3)

Subtracting from 2000, 3000, 4000, 5000, or more thousands

From the above, use the principle of 'last from 10 and the rest from nine' and 'subtracting 1 from the first digit on the left after all the zeros'

Example 1: Work out 3000 – 347

Using the principle of 'last from 10 the rest from nine' and 'subtracting 1 from the first digit on the left after all the zeros'.

We get the answer to be 2653

Example 2: Work out 7000 – 462

Similarly, the answer in this case is 6538.

Typical Question

At a pharmaceutical company a scientist has **10000 Milliliters** of a particular liquid which she uses for her experiments. She uses up **8743 Milliliters** after several experimental tests. How much does she have left?

Method: 1 0 0 0 0

               - 8 7 4 3

                 1 2 5 7

(Take 8 from 9 to give 1, 7 from 9 to give 2, 4 from 9 to give 5 and finally 3 from 10 to give 7) This means the scientist has 1257 milliliters of liquid left.

Multiplying & Dividing by 10, 100 and 1000 (by powers of 10)

You are expected to be familiar with multiplying and dividing numbers by 10, 100, 1000 or any other power of 10

Speed Method: Rule for multiplying whole numbers:

(1) When multiplying a whole number by 10 add a zero at the end of the number.

(2) When multiplying by 100 add two zeros.

(3) When multiplying by 1000 add three zeros

(4) You simply add the number of zeros reflected in the power of 10.

Some examples will illustrate this:

   (1) 45 × 10 = 450 (add 1 zero to 45)

(2) 67 × 100= 6700 (add 2 zeros to 67)

(3) 65 × 1000= 65000 (add 3 zeros to 65)

(4) 65788 × 1000000 = 65788000000 (add 6 zeros to 65788)

Speed Method: Rules for numbers with decimals:

When multiplying by 10, 100, 1000 move the decimal place the appropriate number of places to the right.

(1) 67.5 × 10 = 675 (the decimal point is moved 1 place to the right to give us 675.0 which is the same as 675)

(2) 67.5 × 100 = 6750 (this time move the decimal point two places to the right to give 6750.0 which is the same as 6750)

(3) 6.87 ×1000 = 6870 (in this case move the decimal point three places to the right to give the required answer.)

Now consider examples involving division by 10, 100 and 1000 and other powers of ten.

(1) 450 ÷ 10 = 45 (You simply remove one zero from the number)

(2) 5600 ÷ 100 =56 (This time you remove two zeros from the number)

(3) 45 ÷ 100=0.45 (No zeros to remove – so this time move the decimal point two places to the left to give us 0.45)

(4) 345.78 ÷ 100 =3.4578 (Again simply move the decimal point 2 places to the left to give the answer)

(5) 456.78 ÷ 1000 =0.45678 (Move the decimal point 3 places to the left as shown)

(6) 458 ÷ 0.1 =4580 (remember 0.1 means one–tenth, so dividing a number by 0.1 or one-tenth means the answer becomes 10 times bigger.)

Questions involving powers of 10

(1) Divide 27000 Milliliters by 100

(2) What is78.87 multiplied by 1000?

(3) What is 67 divided by 100?

(4) What is 687 divided by 0.1? (Tip: Dividing by 0.1 is the same as dividing by one tenth, the answer should thus be 10X bigger) **Using the methods shown earlier the answers are:** (1) 270 ml   (2) 78870   (3) 0.67   (4) 6870

If you feel comfortable with the methods above you can skip the traditional method below - although if you have time it will add to your conceptual understanding and will help explain why the 'speed method' leads to the correct answers. If you decide to skip the next bit make sure you look at the last part to do with large and small numbers.

Traditional method of multiplying by 10

The traditional method of multiplying by a 10, 100, 1000 is shown below. This method is useful as it cements the conceptual understanding required. Consider having to work out 34 X 10

Consider place value. For example for the number 34, the right hand digit is the units digit and the number 3 on the left hand side is the tens digit or column. In fact every time you move one place to the left you increase the value by 10. So moving left by one place from the tens column we get the 100's column as shown below.

Hundreds	Tens	Units
	3	4

When we multiply by 10 each digit moves one column to the left. So 34 X 10 =340 as shown below. In other words 3 tens becomes 3 hundreds, the 4 units becomes 4 tens as shown. Also notice we have 0 units so we must put a zero in the units column. Moving each digit 1 place to the left has the effect of making it 10 X bigger.

Hundreds	Tens	Units
3	4	0

Consider the sum 34 X 100

Multiplying by 100 is similar. We simply multiply by 10 and then 10 again. This has the effect of moving each digit two places to the left. This makes it 100 X bigger.

The number 34 is shown below as 3 tens and 4 units.

Thousands	Hundreds	Tens	Units
		3	4

We will now do the multiplication and see its effect.

Clearly multiplying 34 by 100 has the effect of moving the 3 in the tens column to the thousands column and the 4 units to the hundreds column. This is shown below.

Thousands	Hundreds	Tens	Units
3	4	0	0

So 34 X 100 = 3400 as shown above.

This technique is important as it illustrates the concept of multiplying by 10 or 100 taking place. The same process applies to multiplying by 1000, 10,000 or a higher power of 10.

Also note, there is a short hand way of writing 100, 1000, 10,000 and larger powers of 10.

$100 = 10^2$ (10 squared, which is 10 × 10)

$1000 = 10^3$ (10 cubed which is 10 × 10 × 10)

$10,000 = 10^4$ ((10 to the power 4, which is 10 × 10 × 10 × 10)

$1000,000 = 10^6$ (10 to the power 6 which is 10 × 10 × 10 × 10 × 10 × 10)

Higher powers can be written similarly.

Small numbers:

One tenth is $\frac{1}{10}$ = 0.1 but can also be written 10^{-1}

One hundredth $= \frac{1}{100}$ =0.01 which can be written as 10^{-2}

One thousandth $= \frac{1}{1000}$ =0.001 which can be written as 10^{-3}

One millionth $= \frac{1}{1000000}$ =0.000001 which can be written as 10^{-6}

Any small number can be written as power of 10 with a negative sign as shown above. Very small numbers are useful in science, for example in particle physics.

Dividing by 10, 100 and 1000

Conceptually, dividing by 10, 100 or 1000 is a similar process, except, on this occasion, you move the digits to the right by the appropriate number of places.

Consider having to divide 34 by 10.

Here 3 tens and 4 units becomes 3 units and 4 tenths as shown.

Hundreds	Tens	Units	Tenths
		3	4

The rationale for this is that we move each digit to the right. So 3 tens becomes 3 units and 4 units becomes 4 tenths as shown above. The answer is written as 3.4. Similarly, when dividing by 100 or a 1000 the number is moved two and three places to the right as appropriate. We will now look at the technique below to work out the answer mechanically. This ensures you get the right answer without having to resort to the thousands, hundreds, tens, units, tenths and hundredths column. The simple rules shown previously may help those students who find the above process difficult.

Chapter 2   Arithmetic Part 2

Most questions in the numerical reasoning tests will require several steps and include various operations i.e. **+, - , x and ÷**

Time Based Questions

For converting time from 12 hour clock to 24 hour clock - see examples below

12 –Hour Clock	24 –Hour Clock
8.45 am	08:45
11.30 am	11:30
12.20pm	12:20
2.35 pm	14: 35 (after 12pm add the appropriate minutes and hours to 12 hours, in this case 2hrs 35mins +12hrs = 14:35)
8.45 pm	20:45 (8hrs 45mins + 12hrs = 20:45)
11.47pm	23:47 (11hrs 47mins +12hrs = 23:47)

The Convention is that if the time is in 24-hr clock there is no need to put hrs after the time.

Also remember: 2.5 hours = 2 hours 30minutes (0.5 hours = half of 60 minutes)

2.25 hours = Two and a quarter hours = 2hrs 15 minutes

2.4 hours = 2 hours 24 minutes (0.4 hours = 0.4X60 = 24 minutes)

2.1 hours = 2 hours 6 minutes (0.1hours = 0.1 X 60 = 6 minutes)

For other time based questions e.g. years, months, days, hours, minutes or seconds remember the appropriate units.

Example 1: At a company new candidates are mentored once a week for 12 minutes each. There are 15 candidates who are being mentored. There is also a break for 20 minutes in between the mentoring sessions. The session starts at 11.30am. When does it finish? Give your answer using the 24 hour clock

Method: Clearly we need to first work out the total time it takes for all the candidates. Total time for 15 candidates is $15 \times 12 = (15 \times 10 + 15 \times 2) = 180$ minutes = 3 hours plus break time of 20 minutes. So the mentoring session ends 3hrs and 20 minutes after 11.30am – this means it ends at 2.50pm. However using the 24 hour clock the times it ends is 14:50

Example 2: Peter completes a lap in 2.3 minutes. How many minutes and seconds is this?

Convert 0.3 minutes into seconds. Since one whole minute = 60 seconds, then 0.3 minutes = 0.3X60 = 18 seconds. Hence Peter completes the lap in 2 minutes and 18 seconds.

(Note that 0.3 X 60 is the same as 3 X 6, hence this is equivalent to 18)

General Multiplication questions

Example1 There are 4 medium size boxes containing 18 black jumpers each and 3 bigger boxes containing 23 black jumpers each. How many black jumpers are there altogether?

Method: 4 boxes of 18 each imply there are 4 X 18 = 72 black jumpers

(Another way of working out 4 X 18 is to break it down as follows: 4 X 18 = 4 X 10 + 4 X8 = 40 + 32 =72)

Similarly, 3 boxes of 23 each means, 3 X 23 =69 black jumpers

Finally, 72 + 69 = 70 +2 + 60 + 9 = 130 + 11 =141

There are a total of 141 black jumpers altogether

Example2

I buy 5 books for £3.97 each. How much change do I get from a £20 note?

Method: Round up each book to £4. Hence the cost of 5 books = £4X5 – 5X3p = £20 - 15p = £19. 85

You can see straight away that I get 15p change from my £20 note

More multiplication methods that may be helpful

The Grid Method of Multiplication

This is a very powerful method for those who find traditional long multiplication methods difficult.

Example1: Multiply 37 × 6

Re-write the number 37 as 30 and 7 and re-write as shown in the grid table.

$$
\begin{array}{c|cc}
\times & 30 & 7 \\
\hline
6 & 180 & 42
\end{array}
$$

 Now simply add up all the numbers inside the grid. So the answer is 180 + 42 =222

Example 2: work out 15×13

To work this out using the grid method, re-write 15 as 10 and 5, and 13 as 10 and 3 as shown on the outside of the grid table.

$$
\begin{array}{c|cc}
\times & 10 & 5 \\
\hline
10 & 100 & 50 \\
3 & 30 & 15
\end{array}
$$

Multiply out the outside horizontal numbers with the outside vertical numbers to get the numbers inside as shown. Finally, just add up the inside numbers which in this case is 100+50+30+15 =195

Multiplication with decimals

Example3: Work out 1.5 × 1.3

Step1: Leave out the decimal points and just work out the answer to 15×13 as shown above.

We know the answer to this is 195.

Step2: Now count the number of digits there are from the right before the decimal place for each number being multiplied and add them up. That is one for the first number and one for the second number to give a total of 2.

Step3: In the answer 195 count two from the right hand side and insert the decimal point.

So the answer is 1.95

Example 4: Work out 0.15 × 1.3

We know the answer to 15 ×13 is 195

This time the number of digits for each number before the decimal point is 2 for the first number and 1 for the second number giving a total of 3.

We now count 3 places from the right and insert a decimal point.

So the answer is 0.195

If you want to you can think of getting the answer another way:

Consider **Example 3** again: Multiply 1.5×1.3

We know the answer is 210. Note the fact that 1.5 is 15 divided by 10 and 1.3 is 13 divided by 10. So the answer is simply 195 divided by 10 ×10 =100, so we divide 195 by 100 to get the answer as 1.95

More Multiplication

We will look at some fascinating ways of quickly multiplying by 11, 9, and 5, which will help you speed up your number work in mental arithmetic

Multiplying quickly by 11

One common method used is to multiply by 10 and then add the number itself. We will now look at a super- efficient method that is rarely used.

Super-efficient Speed Method:

11 ×11 =121 (the first and last digits remain the same & the middle number is the sum of the first two digits)

The basic method is: Start with the first digit, add the next two, until the last one. This method works with any number of digits.

Let us explore a few more examples with two digit numbers.

13 ×11= 143 (Keep the first and last digit of the number 13 the same, add 1 & 3 to give the middle number 4)

14 × 11= 154

19 × 11= 1(10)9=209 (Notice the middle number is 10, since 1+9=10, so we need to carry 1 to the left hand number.)

A few more examples will show the power of this method.

27 × 11= 297 (the first number=2, the middle number=2+7, the last number =7)

28 × 11=2(10)8= 308 (using similar analysis to 19 × 11 above)

The same principle applies to numbers with more than 2 digits.

Example: Work out 215 × 11

Method: Keep the first and the last digit the same. Starting from the first digit add the subsequent digit to get the next digit, do this again with the second digit until the last digit which stays the same. So, 215 × 11 =2365 (2, is the first digit so stays the same, the sum of 2 and 1 gives you the next digit 3, the sum of 1 and 5 gives you the third digit 6 and finally the last digit 5 stays the same)

Example involving multiplying by 11

In a certain company 54 insurance agents manage to sell 11 insurance policies each in a particular month.

How many insurance policies did these agents sell altogether in that month?

54 × 11 using the method explained above is 594

Hence, total insurance policies sold in this month by these agents = 594 (Method: Keep the first and last digit of the number 54 he same, add 5 & 4 to give the middle number 9)

Multiplying by 5 quickly

Multiply the number by 10 and halve the answer.

Example 1: 5 × 4 = half of 10 × 4 = half of 40 = 20

Example 2: 5 × 16 = half of 10 × 16 = half of 160 =80

Example 3: 5 × 23 = half of 10 × 23 = half of 230 = 115

Multiplying by 9 quickly

Here is an easy method to work out the 9× table

Example 1: Work out 9×7

Method

Step1: Add '0' to the number you are going to multiply by 9, e.g. 7 to get 70

Step2: Now subtract 7 from 70 to get 63 which is the final answer

Example 2: Work out 9 × 35

Method

Step1: Add '0' to the number you are going to multiply by 9, i.e. 35 to get 350

Step2: Now subtract 35 from 350 to get 315 which is the final answer

Example 3: Work out 9 × 78

Method

Step1: Add '0' to the number you are going to multiply by 9, e.g. 78 to get 780

Step2: Now subtract 78 from 780 to get 702 which is the final answer

Multiplying by 12 quickly

Example1: Work out 8 × 12

Method: Multiply 8 by 10 then add to it double of 8

$8 \times 10 = 80$

Double $8 = 16$

$80 + 16 = 96$ hence $8 \times 12 = 96$

Example2: Work out 27×12

First work out 27×10, which equals 270

Now double 27 (or 2×27) = 54

Hence $27 \times 12 = 270 + 54 = 324$

Example 3: Work out 75×12

$75 \times 12 = 750 + 2 \times 75$
$= 750 + 150 = 900$

Hence $75 \times 12 = 900$

The Order of Arithmetical Operations

Remembering the order in which you do arithmetical operations is very

important. The rule taught traditionally is that of **BIDMAS.**

The **BIDMAS** rule is as follows:

 (1) Always work out the **B**racket(s) first
 **(2) Then work out the Indices of a number (squares, cubes, square roots
    and so on)**
 (3) Now **M**ultiply and **D**ivide
 (4) Finally do the **A**ddition and **S**ubtraction.

Example 1: $4 + 13(7 - 2)$ this means add 4 to $13 \times (7 - 2)$

**Do the brackets first so $7 - 2 = 5$, then multiply 5 by 13 to get 65 and finally
add 4 to get 69**

Example 2: Work out 2 + 8×3

Do the multiplication before the addition

So 8×3 =24 and 2 + 24 = 26

Example 3: work out $3^2 \times 5 - 9$

(3^2 means 3×3 or 3 squared)

Work out the **square of 3 first**, then **multiply by 5** and finally **subtract 9** from the result.

So we have 3×3 = 9,   9×5 = 45 and finally 45 - 9 = 36

Summary:

When working out sums involving mixed operations (e.g. +, - , x and ÷) you need to work out the steps in stages using the BIDMAS rule: So to work out 8 +25 ×12

Do the multiplication first, 25×12 =300, write down 300 then add 8 to get the answer 308.

Square numbers between 11 & 19 with ease.

Squaring numbers simply means multiplying the number by itself

So for example 6^2 means 6×6 = 36

(It assumes you know your tables till 12×)

Example1:

Work out the square of 12

Step (1) gives us 14 (Take the last digit of 12, that is 2 and add it to 12)

Step (2) Square the last digit of the original number. So 2X2 = 4

Step (3) Place this answer at the end of 14 in step (1) to get 144

So 12 X 12 = 144

Example 2:

Work out the square of 13.

Step (1) gives us 16 (Simply add the last digit to the number itself)

Step (2) gives us 9 (This was obtained by squaring the last digit of 13, that is 3×3)

Step (3) gives us 169 (we simply place 9 at the end of 16)

So 13 X 13 =169

Example 3:

Work out the square of 14.

Step (1) produces 18

Step (2) gives us 16

Step (3) Produces   18 $_1$ 6

(Carry the '1' to the 'tens' digit on the left)

That means '1' has now to be added to 18 to produce 196 as the final answer.

Example 4:

Work out the square of 15.

Step (1) produces 20

Step (2) Produces 25

Step (3) Produces   20 $_2$ 5

 (Carry the '2' to the 'tens' digit on the left)

That means '2' has now to be added to 20 to produce 225 as the final answer.

See if you can work out 16 X 16, 17 X 17, 18 X 18 and 19 X 19

An elegant method of squaring numbers ending in 5

As you probably know by now that squaring is simply multiplying a number itself.

15^2 means 15×15

Example 1: Work out 15×15

The answer has two parts. If the numbers to be multiplied each end in 5, then the last part is always 25. The first part is the first digit multiplied by 'one more'. In this case this is 1 X 2=2. So the first part is 2. The answer is thus 225.

Another two examples will help consolidate this method.

Example 2: Work out 25×25

As before, the answer has two parts. The last part is always 25. The first part is the first digit multiplied by 'one more'. In this case this is $2 \times 3=6$. So the first part is 6. The answer is thus 625

Example 3: Work out 65×65

The first part is $6 \times 7= 42$ (Since the first digit is 6 and multiplying it by 'one more' makes it 6×7). The second part as before is 25. The answer is thus 4225

This method works with any two same digit numbers ending in 5. So for example 115×115

The answer has two parts. The last part is 25. The first part is 11×12 (first two digit number multiplied by 'one more'). The first part is thus 132. Hence, 115 ×115= 13225.

Try squaring a big number such as: 9995×9995

Last part is 25. The first part is $999 \times 1000=999000$. The answer is thus 99900025

Multiplication when all the digits before the last digit are the same and the last digits add up to 10 – This is an extension of the previous method

Example 1: Work out 32 × 38 (Notice the first digit for each number is the same and the last digits add up to 10)

As before the answer is in two parts. The last part is simply the last digit of each number multiplied together and the first part is the first digit multiplied by one more. In this case the last part is 2 X 8=16. The first part is 3 X 4=12. So the answer is 1216

Example 2: work out 56 × 54

(Note that the first digit of each part of the sum is the same, namely, 5 and the last digit of each part of the sum adds up to 10 that is 6+4=10)

.The answer is in two parts. The last part is simply 6 X 4=24 and the first part is 5 times 'one more'. This makes it 5 X 6=30. Hence the answer is 3024

Three more examples will help consolidate this method.

Example 3: Work out 78 × 72

The last part is 8 × 2=16

The first part is 7 × 8=56 (first number times 'one more')

Hence the answer is 5616

Example 4: Work out 123 × 127

The last part is 3 × 7 =21

The first part is 12 × 13 (first number in this case is 12)=156

Hence the answer is 15621.

Example 5: Work out 9996 × 9994

The last part is 6 × 4=24

The first part is 999 × 1000=999000

Hence the answer is 99900024

We can see that this is a really powerful method of multiplication for this special case of numbers.

Division

In general the traditional short division approach is a good method. However, there are some other smart techniques worth considering for special situations.

Dividing a number by 2 is a very useful skill, since if you can divide by 2, you can by halving it again divide by 4 and halving it again divide by 8.

Dividing by 2, 4 and 8

Simply halve the number to divide by 2

(Some find it difficult to halve a number like 13. An alternative strategy is to multiply the number by 5 and divide by 10)

Halving again is the same as dividing by 4

And halving once more is the same as dividing by 8

Example 1: $28 \div 2 = 14$

Example 2: $268 \div 4 = 134 \div 2 = 67$

Example 3: $568 \div 8 = 284 \div 4 = 142 \div 2 = 71$

Example 4: $65 \div 4 = 32.5 \div 2 = 16.25$

Dividing by 5

An easy way to do this is to multiply the number by 2 and divide by 10.

Example 1: $120 \div 5 = (120 \times 2) \div 10 = 240 \div 10 = 24$

Example 2: $127 \div 5 = (127 \times 2) \div 10 = 254 \div 10 = 25.4$

Similarly to divide by 50 simply multiply by 2 and divide by 100

Dividing by 25

A good way to do this is to multiply by 4 and divide by 100.

Example1: $240 \div 25 = (240 \times 4) \div 100 = 960 \div 100 = 9.6$

Example2: $700 \div 25 = (700 \times 4) \div 100 = 2800 \div 100 = 28$

Dividing by other numbers: The conventional short division method is a good method but you might find the speed methods below useful sometimes.

Question involving division

Example1: In one particular week in a restaurant a bonus of £67.50 is divided amongst three waiters. How much does each one get in that week?

Clearly this is the same as $60 \div 3$ added to $7.5 \div 3$

$60 \div 3 = 20$ and $7.5 \div 3 = 2.5$ which altogether is 22.5

Hence, £67.5 $\div$ 3 =£22.50 per waiter

Calculators are always there to do complicated divisions like 22.567÷ 3.456

However for everyday life it is useful to know how to do simple divisions with speed.

Example 1: Divide 145 by 7

(145 = 140 + 5)

We can say that $140 \div 7 = 20$, and then we are left with 5/7.

So the answer is 20 and $\frac{5}{7}$ or $20\frac{5}{7}$

Example 2: Divide 103 by 9

$(103 = 99 + 4)$

$= 99 \div 9 + 4/9$

$= 11\frac{4}{9}$

Example 3: Work out 3215 ÷3

$3215 = 3000 + 210 + 5$

So $\dfrac{3215}{3} = \dfrac{3000}{3} + \dfrac{210}{3} + \dfrac{5}{3} = 1000 + 70 + 1\frac{2}{3} = 1071\frac{2}{3}$

Rounding numbers and estimating

We will start simply with rounding numbers to the nearest 10 and 100

Consider the number 271

Rounded to the nearest 10 this number is 270

Rounded to the nearest 100 this number is 300

(The principle is that if the right hand digit is lower than 5 you drop this number and replace it by 0. Conversely if the number is 5 or more drop that digit and add 1 to the left)

Try a few more:

5382 to the nearest 10 is 5380

5382 to the nearest hundred is 5400

5382 to the nearest 1000 is 5000

This rule can also be applied to decimal numbers:

3.7653 rounded to the nearest thousandth is 3.765

3.7653 rounded to the nearest hundredth is 3.77

3.7653 rounded to the nearest tenth is 3.8

3.7653 rounded to the nearest unit is 4

Tip: remember to use common sense when rounding in real life situations:

Example: A book store wants to keep 120 books in the same size boxes. They can fit 22 books in a box. How many boxes will they need?

Method: Number of boxes required will be 120÷22= 5.5 (to one decimal place). But clearly, they cannot have 5.5 boxes. So they need to have 6 boxes

Estimating calculations quickly

Example 1: Work out (2.2 × 7.12)/4.12

We can quickly estimate that this is roughly equal to (2 X 7)/4 =14/4 which is around 3.5 or 4 rounded to the nearest unit. The actual answer is: 3.8 (to 1 decimal place)

Example 2: Work out 38 × 2.9 × 0.53

We can approximate 38 to be 40 to the nearest ten

We can approximate 2.9 o 3 to the nearest unit

We can approximate 0.53 to 0.5 to the nearest tenth

So the magnitude of the answer is 40 × 3 × 0.5

This is 120 × 0.5 =60 (approximately)

Chapter 3   Arithmetic Part 3

Fractions, decimals and percentages

I am sure most of you are aware that $\frac{1}{2}$ = 0.5. This in turn is equal to 50%.

It is worth reviewing this fact. In addition, you should try and remember the following other equivalences if you have forgotten them.

Fractions, decimals and percentage equivalents

Fractions	Decimal	Percentage
$\frac{1}{2}$	0.5	50%
$\frac{1}{4}$	0.25	25%
$\frac{3}{4}$	0.75	75%
$\frac{1}{10}$	0.1	10%
$\frac{1}{5}$	0.2	20%

If we know $\frac{1}{2}$ = **0.5**

We can deduce that $\frac{1}{4}$ = **0.25**

(Since a quarter is half of half)

Similarly $\frac{1}{8}$ is **0.125**

We can do this quickly because all we do is halve each decimal value.

Half of 0.5 is 0.25, Half of 0.25 is 0.125

We can of course continue this process.

Further if we know $\frac{1}{10}$ =0.1 we can now work out $\frac{2}{10}, \frac{3}{10}, \frac{7}{10}$ etc.

$\frac{2}{10} = 0.2$ **(2 × 0.1),** $\frac{3}{10} = 0.3$ **(3 × 0.1,** $\frac{7}{10} = 0.7$ **(7 × 0.1),** $\frac{9}{10} = 0.9$ **(9 × 0.1)**

**Another useful fraction and decimal equivalent to remember is $\frac{1}{3}$ =0.333...
(0.3 recurring)**

The key equivalent percentages to remember are as follows:

$\frac{3}{4} = 75\%$**,** $\frac{1}{2} = 50\%$**,** $\frac{1}{4} = 25\%$**,** $\frac{1}{8} = 12.5\%$**,** $\frac{1}{10} = 10\%$

See summary box below

Summary:

Remember the following equivalences

$\frac{1}{2}$ **=0.5** **=50%,** $\frac{1}{4}$ **=0.25 =25%,** $\frac{3}{4}$ **=0.75 =75%,** $\frac{1}{10}$ **=0.1=10%**

Also if you can try to remember, $\frac{1}{5}$ **=0 .2 = 20%, and** $\frac{2}{5}$ **=0.4 =40%,** $\frac{1}{3}$ **=0.333...
(0.3 recurring) = 33.33% (to 2 decimal places)**

To convert a fraction into a percentage, simply multiply the fraction by 100

Questions involving percentages and fractions

Example 1: Find 25% of £250

Method: Find 50% of £250 and halve it again.

Half of £250 = £125, Half of £125 =£62.50, so 25% of £250 = £62.50

Example 2: In a marketing department of 25 people there are 12 women and the rest are men.

(1) What fraction of the marketing department consists of men?

(2) What percentage is this?

(1) Since there are 12 women, there are 13 men out of 25. So the fraction of men is $\frac{13}{25}$

(2) The percentage of men is $\frac{13}{25}$ × 100 = 52%, (Divide 100 by 25 to get 4. Then multiply 13 by 4 to get 52%)

Example 3: 30% of the applicants for a certain job are male. There are 30 candidates in total. How many of the applicants are female?

Method: If 30% of the applicants are male, this means 70% are female. So we need to find 70% of 30 candidates. Since 10% of 30 is 3, this means 70% corresponds to 3X7 = 21 females. Hence, 21 of the candidates are female.

Working out increase or decrease in percentages from original value

Example1: In a certain corner shop 16 packs of cereal A were sold in week 1. In the same shop 20 packs of the same cereal were sold in week 2. What was the percentage increase in the cereal packs A sold from week 1 to week 2?

Method: Increase in number of cereal packs A = 20 – 16 =4. Original number of cereal packs =16. The increase of 4 was based on 16 cereal packs. To work out the percentage increase we simply divide the increase by the original number of cereal packs and multiply this by 100. That is $\frac{4}{16} \times 100 = \frac{1}{4} \times 100 = 25\%$

To work out decrease in percentages (uses the same principle as above)

Example2: The original price of a projector was: £150, the new price is reduced to £135. What is the percentage decrease in price? The decrease in price is £150 - £135 = £15. The decrease over the original price is $\frac{15}{150}$. To turn this into a percentage we multiply $\frac{15}{150} \times 100 = \frac{1500}{150} = 10\%$. So the decrease in percentage price is 10%.

The basic formula to work out increase or decrease percentage change is shown below:

$$\frac{difference\ between\ final\ and\ original\ value}{original\ value} \times 100$$

One thing to remember though is that the increase or decrease in percentage points is different from **increase or decrease in percentages.**

To illustrate this consider the example below:

The unemployment rate in a region A was 8% in 2010. In 2011 the unemployment rate in the same region was 10%. **(1)** What was the **percentage point** increase in unemployment from 2010 to2011? **(2)** What is the **percentage increase** in unemployment from 2010 to 2011?

(1) The **percentage point** increase is simply 2% (i.e. from 8% to 10%)

(2) However the **percentage increase** in unemployment is $\frac{2}{8} \times 100 = \frac{200}{8} = \frac{100}{4} = $ 25%.

In the Numerical reasoning test context, if you are asked to work out the **percentage point increase,** say in sales in Product A changing from 20% to 30%. The answer is obviously 10%. But if asked to work out the **percentage increase**, then the answer is $\frac{10}{20} \times 00 = \frac{1000}{20} = \frac{100}{2} = 50\%$

Miscellaneous questions involving fractions and percentages

Example 1: Finding fraction of an amount

Find $\frac{3}{4}$ of £600, First find $\frac{1}{2}$ = £300, then find $\frac{1}{4}$ (which is half of half) = £150

Therefore $\frac{3}{4}$ = £450 (adding half plus a quarter)

Example 2: Finding a fraction and turning it into a percentage

There are 40 builders in a small town in Yorkshire. In a particular month 5 builders are without work.

What is the percentage of builders that do not have work in this month in this small town?

The fraction of builders without work = $\frac{5}{40}$, by dividing top and bottom numbers by 5 we get $\frac{1}{8}$

To convert 1/8 into a percentage simply multiply 1/8 by 100

= 1/8 X100 =100/8 = 50/4 =25/2 =12.5%

(Another method: We know ¼ =25%

Hence 1/8 =12.5% (Since 1/8 is half of a quarter)

Calculator based questions

You need to remember that percent means out of 100. That is $\frac{1}{100}$. So to find say 42.5% of a number, divide the number by 100 and multiply it by 42.5.

Example: work out 42.5% of £400

We can say that this is the same as (£400 ÷ 100) × 42.5 =4 × 42.5 = £170

Try working this out with a basic calculator to see if you agree with the answer.

Do the calculations in steps. For example to work out 3.65 + 15×6

Use the rule that you always do multiplication and division before you do addition and subtraction. So to work out 3.65 +15×6, we work out 15×6 first. This gives us 90, then we add 3.65 to 90 to give us 93.65 as the final answer. Note to clear the answer simply click on [C] on the calculator.

Simple Interest and Compound Interest

Simple Interest

Example 1: I have £5000 in a building society account which pays me simple interest of 3% per annum. I keep my money for 3 years. How much in total will I have at the end of the 3 year period?

Method: At the end of the first year the total interest I will receive is 3% of £5000. This is $3\dfrac{3}{100} X 5000 = \dfrac{15000}{100} = £150$ per annum.

At the end of 3 years I will receive 3X £150 = £450 total interest. This means the total amount I will have is £5450 (original £5000 plus 3 years of simple interest)

You can if you like use the formula below to work out the total simple interest over a given period of time.

I =PRT where I = Total interest, P = Principal amount (original amount), R is the annual interest rate and T = the time in years.

So in the above case I =$5000 X \dfrac{3}{100} X 3 = £5000 \times \dfrac{9}{100} = £450$

Finally, to find the total amount we have at the end of the 3 year period, we simply add £450 to the original £5000 to get £5450

Example 2: Work out the final amount at the end of one year if there is a 10% increase per annum and I have $3000 to start with.

The traditional method is to work out 10% of $3000 first. Then add this answer to $3000 to get the final answer.

So 10% of $3000 = $300. So the final price after a 10% increase is $3000 + $300 =$3300

Here is fast and efficient method to work out the final price:

Simply work out 1.1× 000

Since 1.1 denotes a 10% increase.

Why 1.1? Since 100% plus 10% =1 + 0.1 = 1.1

Now 1.1× 3000 = $3300 which is the final answer

Compound Interest (you can use a calculator to work out the examples below!)

Now consider a problem involving recurring percentage changes

Example 1

Find the value of $5000 if I gain a profit of 10% the first year followed by (10% of the new amount) in the second year. (This is called compound interest)

THIS MEANS THE INCREASE IS 1.1× FOLLOWED BY 1.1× AGAIN

Or $(1.1)^2 \times 5000$

$(1.1)^2 \times 5000 = 1.21× 5000 = 6050

So the final value is $6050

Example 2

I buy a one bedroom apartment for $200,000. It increases in value by 5% per annum

How much will it be worth in 15 years?

Method: Increase after 1 year will be 1.05X$200,000, after two years it will be: $(1.05)^2 \times $200,000$, after three years it will be $(1.05)^3 \times $200,000$. So, after 15 years it will be worth $(1.05)^{15} \times $200,000 = 415786

Example 4:

A car depreciates by 30% per annum. I buy it at £18000. What is its value in 5 years' time? Give your answer to the nearest pound

Method:

After one year its value will decrease by 30%, so its new value will be 70% of original as shown below:

£18000×0.7, hence, after five years its value will be $18000× $(0.7)^5$

Value after five years is £3025

Example 5:

I have a house that is currently valued at £300,000. House prices are predicted to fall 7% per annum for the next two years followed by a 5% growth for a subsequent five years. What is the value of my house after seven years?

Method:

The value of my house changes by 'depreciating' for two years followed by 'appreciating' for the subsequent five years.

So the value is £300000 × $(0.93)^2$ × $(1.05)^5$

= £331157 (to the nearest pound)

(Note: 0.93 denotes the depreciation by 7%, and 1.05 denotes the growth by 5%)

Chapter 4   Arithmetic Part 4   Fractions

Simplifying fractions

Reducing a fraction to its lowest terms

Basically you need to find numbers that divide into the top number (numerator) as well as the bottom number (denominator), and then divide them both by the same number (start with 2, if doesn't go then choose 3, then 5, and then the next prime factor e.g. 7, 11, etc.)

Example1: Reduce $\frac{16}{24}$ to its lowest terms.

8 divides exactly into 16 and 24, so in the fraction $\frac{16}{24}$ divide top and bottom by 8. This gives the answer as $\frac{2}{3}$

In case you can't see this straight away, try starting with the number two and work your way numerically upwards using the next prime factor i.e. try 3, then 5 etc. if required

So for the fraction $\frac{16}{24}$ we can start dividing top and bottom by 2 to give us $\frac{8}{12}$, then do the same again as both 8 and 12 are still divisible by 2. This gives us $\frac{4}{6}$ and finally repeating the process once more reduces the fraction to $\frac{2}{3}$ which is the simplest form.

Example 2: Simplify $\frac{9}{12}$ to its lowest terms

In this case we can't divide top and bottom by 2, so we try 3. Since 3 will go into both 9 and 12, we can reduce this to the fraction $\frac{3}{4}$ (since 9 ÷3 =3 and 12 ÷ 3 =4), Hence, $\frac{9}{12}$ reduces to $\frac{3}{4}$

Example 3: Reduce fraction $\frac{49}{77}$ to its lowest terms. This time we need to spot that 2, 3, 5, does not go into either 49, or 77. Either by trial and error or by spotting the right number we notice 7 goes into both the numerator and the denominator. This reduces

$\frac{49}{77}$ to $\frac{7}{11}$

> **Cancelling down fractions to its simplest form (lowest terms)**
>
> **To simplify a fraction to its lowest terms you divide the numerator and the denominator by the same prime factors (2, 3, 5, 7, 11, etc.) to give the equivalent fractions as shown in the examples above**

Finding fraction of an amount

Example1: Find $\frac{2}{5}$ of 25, simply replace the 'of' by X. (times)

So $\frac{2}{5}$ of 25 becomes $\frac{2}{5}$ X 25

To work this out find out 1/5 of 25 and then multiply the answer by 2. So 25 divided by 5, equals 5, then 2 x 5 =10. Hence $\frac{2}{5}$ of 25 =10

> **Example:**
>
> 60 people apply for a certain job vacancy. 12 people are short-listed for an interview. What is the proportion of people that are not short listed for the interview? Give your answer as a decimal.
>
> Total number of people applying for this job = 60. Since 12 people are shortlisted, this means 48 are not shortlisted. Hence the proportion that is not shortlisted = 48/60. If you divide top and bottom by 6, this simplifies to 8/10.
>
> The answer as a decimal is 0.8

Adding and Subtracting Fractions

This next section will help you revise adding, subtracting, multiplying and dividing fractions together

Consider adding and subtracting fractions together.

When the bottom numbers (denominators) are the same, just add the top numbers together keeping the bottom number the same, likewise for subtraction just subtract the top two numbers.

Example 1: $\frac{2}{5}$ + $\frac{1}{5}$ = $\frac{3}{5}$

Example 2: $\dfrac{2}{5}$ - $\dfrac{1}{5}$ = $\dfrac{1}{5}$

When the denominators are different

Example 3: Work out $\dfrac{1}{2}$ + $\dfrac{2}{5}$

When the denominators are different, the traditional method of doing this is to find the lowest common denominator. We have to find a number that both 2 and 5 will go into. This is clearly 10.

We can now re-write the fraction with the same common denominator.

To do this we have to ask how did we get the denominator from 2 to 10 for the first part, and likewise for the second part from 5 to 10. The answer is shown below:

$$\dfrac{1X5}{2X5} + \dfrac{2X2}{5X2} = \dfrac{5}{10} + \dfrac{4}{10} = \dfrac{9}{10}$$

We had to multiply top and bottom by 5 for the first part and top and bottom by 2 for the second part as shown above. We can then add the fraction as we have the same common denominator.

We can however use another very simple strategy that always works. The method is that of crosswise multiplication.

The basic method is to take the fraction sum and do crosswise multiplication as shown by the arrows. In addition, multiply the denominators (bottom numbers) together to get the new denominator.

Example 1: $\dfrac{1}{2}$ ✕ $\dfrac{2}{5}$ = $\dfrac{1X5+2X2}{2X5}$ = $\dfrac{5+4}{10}$ = $\dfrac{9}{10}$

We notice that if we cross multiply as shown we get 1 X 5 and 2 X 2 respectively at the top. To get the bottom number we simply multiply the bottom numbers, 2 and 5 together. So the denominator is 2 X 5=10.

Let us try another example:

Example 2: Work out $\dfrac{3}{7}$ + $\dfrac{2}{5}$

Using crosswise multiplication and adding rule, as well as multiplying the bottom two numbers we get:

$$\frac{3}{7} \times \frac{2}{5} = \frac{3X5+7X2}{35} = \frac{15+14}{35} = \frac{29}{35}$$

This is a very elegant method which always works

Example3: Work out $\frac{3}{7} - \frac{2}{5}$

This is similar to the above except instead of adding we now subtract as shown below.

$$\frac{3}{7} \times \frac{2}{5} = \frac{3X5-7X2}{35} = \frac{15-14}{35} = \frac{1}{35}$$

Note: In fact you can use this method when adding or subtracting any fraction that you find difficult. Even if you use this method for simple cases, you will still get the right answer but you may have to cancel down to get the lowest terms for the final answer.

For example we know that $\frac{1}{4} + \frac{1}{2} = \frac{3}{4}$

But if we didn't know and used the method shown we would get $\frac{1}{4} \times \frac{1}{2} =$ $\frac{1X2+4X1}{4X2} = \frac{2+4}{8} = \frac{6}{8} = \frac{3}{4}$ (we get this by dividing both the numerator and denominator in $\frac{6}{8}$ by 2). So we get the same answer in the end

Question involving fractions

(1) Find $2\frac{3}{4}$ of £64

We first work out 2 X 64 = 128, to work out three quarters of 64 we first work out a half and then add it to a quarter of 64.

Half of £64 is £32

A quarter of £64 (is half of £32) is £16

Hence three quarters of £64 = £32 + £16 = £48

So two and three quarters of £64 = £128 + £48 = £176

Adding and subtracting mixed numbers

We first add or subtract the whole numbers and then the fractional parts.

Ex1: $2\frac{2}{5} + 4\frac{3}{7}$

Adding the whole numbers we get 6. (Simply add 2 and 4)

Now add the fractional parts to get: $\frac{14+15}{35} = \frac{29}{35}$

So the answer is $6\frac{29}{35}$

Ex2: $4\frac{3}{7} - 2\frac{2}{5}$

Subtract the whole numbers and then the fractional parts, which gives us:

$2\frac{15-14}{35} = 2\frac{1}{35}$

Multiplying Fractions

Multiplying fractions by the traditional method is quite efficient so we will consider only this approach.

Example 1: $\frac{2}{3} \times \frac{5}{7} = \frac{10}{21}$ In this case we simply multiply the top two numbers to

get the new numerator and multiply the bottom two numbers together to get the new denominator, as shown above.

Another example will help consolidate this process:

Example 2: $\frac{10}{21} \times \frac{5}{7} = \frac{50}{147}$

(Multiply 10 × 5 to get 50 for the numerator and 21 × 7 to get 147 for the denominator)

Division of Fractions

When dividing fractions we invert the second fraction and multiply as shown.

Think of an obvious example. If we have to divide ½ by ¼ we intuitively know that the answer is 2. The reason for this is that there are 2 quarters in one half. Let us see how this works in practice.

Example 1: $\dfrac{1}{2} \div \dfrac{1}{4} = \dfrac{1}{2} \times \dfrac{4}{1} = \dfrac{4}{2} = 2$

Step 1: Re-write fraction as a multiplication sum with the second fraction inverted.

Step 2: Work out the fraction as a normal multiplication

Step 3: Simplify if possible. In this case 4 divided by 2 is 2.

Example 2: $\dfrac{6}{11} \div \dfrac{5}{11} = \dfrac{6}{11} \times \dfrac{11}{5} = \dfrac{66}{55} = \dfrac{6}{5} = 1\dfrac{1}{5}$

Step1: Re-write the fraction inverting the second fraction as shown

Step2: Multiply the top part and the bottom part to get $\dfrac{66}{55}$ as shown.

Step 3: Simplify this by dividing top and bottom by 11 to get $\dfrac{6}{5}$. Now this finally simplifies to $1\dfrac{1}{5}$ as shown.

The following steps are required to convert a mixed number into a fraction. Consider the mixed fraction $2\dfrac{1}{4}$.

Step 1: Multiply the denominator of the fractional part by the whole number and add the numerator. In this case this works out to 2 × 4 + 1 = 9. This now becomes the new numerator.

Step 2: The denominator stays the same as before. Now re-write the new fraction as $\dfrac{9}{4}$. (That is the new numerator ÷ existing denominator)

Let us look at another example. Convert the mixed number, $3\frac{3}{7}$ into a fraction.

Step 1: Multiply denominator of fractional part by whole number and add the numerator.

This gives $3 \times 7+3 = 24$ as the new numerator.

Step2: Re-write fraction as new fraction. This is now the new numerator ÷ existing denominator. This gives us $\frac{24}{7}$

Multiplying mixed numbers together

Consider the examples below:

Example: $1\frac{1}{5} \times 1\frac{3}{8}$

The method is simply to convert both mixed numbers into fractions and multiply as shown below:

$$1\frac{1}{5} \times 1\frac{3}{8} = \frac{6}{5} \times \frac{11}{8} = \frac{66}{40} = 1\frac{26}{40} = 1\frac{13}{20}$$

(Notice $\frac{26}{40}$ simplifies to $\frac{13}{20}$)

Dividing mixed numbers together

Example: $1\frac{1}{2} \div 1\frac{1}{4}$

There are two steps required to work out the division of mixed numbers.

Step1: Convert both mixed numbers into fractions as before

Step 2: Multiply the fractions together but invert the second one.

$$1\frac{1}{2} \div 1\frac{1}{4} = \frac{3}{2} \div \frac{5}{4} = \frac{3}{2} \times \frac{4}{5} = \frac{12}{10} = 1\frac{2}{10} = 1\frac{1}{5}$$

Chapter 5   Proportions and ratios

Although proportion and ratio are related they are not the same thing – see example below for clarification.

Example: In a class there are 15 girls and 10 boys. The **ratio of girls to boys is** 15:10, or 3:2, (divide both 15 and 10 by 5) and the **proportion of girls in the class** is 15 out of 25, $\frac{15}{25}$ **which simplifies to** $\frac{3}{5}$

Questions based on proportions and ratios

Example 1: In a class of 27 pupils, 9 go home for lunch. What is the proportion of pupils in this class that have lunch at school?

Since 9 out of 27 pupils go home, this means 18 pupils have lunch at school.

As a proportion this is 18 out of 27 or $\frac{18}{27}$ **which simplifies to** $\frac{2}{3}$

Example 2: In a certain work place the ratio of males to females is 2: 3 there are 250 workers altogether. How many of these are male?

Step 1: Find out the total number of parts. You can do this by adding up the ratio parts together. E.g. 2:3 means there are (2+3) = 5 parts altogether. This means 1 part = one fifth of 250 workers = 50 workers.

Since the ratio of male to female is 2:3, there are 2X50 males and 3X50 females

The number of males in this workplace =2X50 = 100

Example 3: $100 is divided in the ratio 1: 4 how much is the bigger part?

The total number of parts that $100 is divided into is 5 (to find the number of parts simply add the numbers in the ratio, which in this case is 1 and 4)

Clearly, 1 part equals $20 (100 divided by 5), so 4 parts is equal to $80. This is the required bigger part.

Example 4: $1500 is divided in the ratio of 3 : 5 : 7

Find out how much the smallest part is worth?

Clearly $1500 is divided into a total of 15 Parts

So each part is worth $100 ($1500 divided by 15)

So 3 parts (this is the smallest part) equals $300

Example 5: Two lengths are in the ratio 3: 5. If the first length is 150m what is the second length?

If the ratio is 3: 5 then the lengths are in the ratio 150: n

We now need to determine n. We can see that 150 is 50 times 3.

So, n (which is the second length) must be 50 times 5, which equals 250m.

Example 6: As we have seen, sometimes ratios are expressed in ways, which may not be the simplest form. Consider 5:10

   (a) You can re-write 5:10 as 1:2 (divide both sides by 5)

   (b) 4 : 10 can be re-written as 2 : 5

   (c) 8 : 60 can be re-written as 4 : 30 which, simplifies to 2 : 15

   (d) 15 : 36 simplifies to 5 : 12 (divide both sides by 3)

Example 7: A team of 10 people can deliver 6000 leaflets in a residential estate in 4 hours. How long does it take 6 people to deliver these leaflets?

   Method: 1 person will take 10 times as long or 4X10 = 40hours

This means 6 people will take 40÷6 =20 ÷3 = $6\frac{2}{3}$ hours = 6 hours and 40 minutes. (Since 1/3 of an hour = 20 minutes)

Scales and ratios

Consider that you are reading a map and the scale ratio is 1: 100000

(This means for every one cm on the map the actual distance is 100000 cm or, put another way every one cm on the map, the distance = 1000 m (divide 100000 by 100. To get the result in metres) now, 1000 m = 1km (divide 1000 by 1000 to get 1 since 1km =1000m)

(Scales can also be used in other areas such as architectural drawings)

Question based on scales

I note that the map I am using has a scale of 1: 25000. The distance between the two places I am interested in is 12cm. What is the actual distance in km?

Method: 12 cm on the map corresponds to 12 x 25000 = 300x 1000 =300000cm

=3000m = 3km

(300000 /100 to convert to metres = 3000 m, now divide 3000 by 1000 to convert to km)

Hence the distance between the two places is 3km

Conversions

Conversions are often useful in changing currencies for example from pounds to dollars or euros and vice-versa. It is also useful to convert distances from miles to kilometers or weights from kilograms to pounds and so on. Basically a conversion involves changing information from one unit of measurement to another. Consider some examples below:

Question based on conversions

Example 1: I go to France with £150 and convert this into Euros at 1.2 Euros to a pound.

(1) How many Euros do I get? **(2)** I am left with 39 Euros when I get back home. The exchange rate remains the same. How many pounds do I get back?

Method: (1) Since 1 pound = 1.2 Euros, I get 150 X 1.2 =180 Euros in total. **(2)** When I get back I change 39 Euros back into pounds. This time I need to divide 39 by 1.2

So 39÷1.2 =32.5. This means I get back £32.50

Example 2

The formula for changing kilometers to miles is given by:

M = $\frac{5}{8}$ X **K.** Use this formula to convert 68 kilometers to miles

Method: substitute **K** with 68 and multiply by $\frac{5}{8}$

This means M = $\frac{5}{8}$ X 68. Using a calculator this comes to 42.5 miles

It is worth reviewing some common Metric and Imperial Measures as shown below

Metric Measures

1000 Millilitres (ml) =1 Litre(l)

100 Centilitres (cl) =1 Litre (l)

10ml =1 cl

1 Centimetre (cm) =10 Millimetres (mm)

1 Metre (m) = 100 cm

1 Kilometre (km) =1000 m

1 Kilogram (kg) =1000 grams (g)

Imperial Measurements

1 foot =12 inches

1 yard =3 feet

1 pound = 16 ounces

1 stone =14 pounds (lb)

1 gallon = 8 pints

1 inch = 2.54 cm (approximately)

Question on conversions

A ramblers' group, go on a walking tour whilst in the South of France. They walk from Perpignan to Canet Plage which is approximately 11 km away. After a lunch break and some time on the beach, they walk back to Perpignan. How many miles in total do they walk on that day? (You are given that 8 km is approximately equal to 5 miles.) Give your answer as a decimal.

Method: Total distance walked = 22Km (11 + 11). To convert this into miles we have to multiply 22 by 5 and then divide by 8 (Since 8 km = 5 miles)

That is $22 \times \dfrac{5}{8}$ =13.75 miles (simply multiply 22 by 5 and divide the answer by 8)

(Remember, use of calculator would be allowed for this type of question)

Chapter 6   Formulas

Formula

A formula describes the relationship between two or more variables. Consider a simple case first.

Example 1: A company pays 40p per mile and certain meal expenses when their sales employees visit clients. The cost of claiming mileage is calculated using the formula given, payable at 40p per mile and a fixed cost of £25. The formula is C = M× 0.4 + 25, where C represents the cost in pounds payable to the employee by the company.

So for example if an employee has to travel 40 miles from her home to the client, the employee can claim 80 miles altogether for the journey to the client and back + £25 as shown below by the formula.

Using the formula we have C = 0.4× 80 + 25 = 32 + 25 = £57

(Explanation of working out: Using BIDMAS we multiply before adding. So 0.4×80 =32, finally add 32 and 25 together to get 57)

Example 2:

(1) The formula for working out the distance depends on the speed and time taken in the appropriate units.

D = S×T where D is the distance, S the speed and T is the time.

What is the distance travelled if my speed is 60kmh and I travel for 1hour and 30 minutes.

1 hour 30 minutes corresponds to 1.5 hours so, using the formula, D = 60×1.5 = 90 km

That is, the distance equals 90km

(2) The formula for working out the speed is given as Speed= Distance/Time

That is S = D÷T

Work out the average speed with which I travel, if I cover 100 miles in 2.5 hours.

Since S = D÷T, this means S = 100÷2.5 =40 mph (Notice the units for the first example were in kilometres and units for the second example were in miles

(3) The formula for working out time taken is given by T = D÷S

Calculate the time taken to cover 90 miles if I travel at 60mph?

Time taken, T= D÷S, so T = 90÷60 = 9÷6 =3÷ 2 = 1.5 hours or 1 hour and 30 minutes.

Example 3

The formula for converting the temperature from Celsius to Fahrenheit is given by the formula: $F= \frac{9}{5}C +32$ (where C is the temperature in degrees Centigrade)

If the temperature is 10 degrees Celsius then what is the equivalent in temperature in Fahrenheit?

Using the formula $F= \frac{9}{5}C +32$, and substituting 10 in place of C, we have $F= \frac{9}{5} \times 10 +32 = \frac{90}{5}+ 32 =18+32 =50$. Hence, 10 degrees centigrade = 50 degrees Fahrenheit

(**Explanation of working out above**: Remember we multiply and divide before adding and subtracting) There are no brackets to worry about. When working out $\frac{9}{5}$ X 10 +32, multiply 9 by 10 to get 90, divide this by 5 to get 18, finally add 18 and 32 together to get 50

Example 4: Convert 68 degrees Fahrenheit to degrees Celsius. The formula for converting the temperature from Fahrenheit to Celsius is given by:

$C= \frac{5}{9}(F-32)$. To change 68 degrees Fahrenheit to degrees Celsius we can substitute for F in the formula $C= \frac{5}{9}(F-32)$., C = $C= \frac{5}{9}(68-32)$. =5 X 36/9 = 5 X 4 =20

Hence, 68 degrees Fahrenheit =20 degrees Celsius

(**Explanation of the working out above**: Using BIDMAS we work out the bracket first. This gives us 68-32 =36. We now divide this by 9 and multiply by 5. Clearly 36÷9 =4 and finally 5X4 =20)

We have seen that formulas can be important in conversion problems

Earlier we saw the formula: S = D ÷T, that is, Speed = $\frac{Distance}{Time}$. Sometimes in the On screen questions you may be shown a distance time graph for a school coach trip and asked to work out average speed for a particular part of the journey and the time the coach was stationary. See example below

Example: A school trip by coach to a heritage site leaves at 1200 hrs from the school. The coach arrives at the destination at 1300hrs. It then stops so the pupils can look around the site. Finally after looking around the site it leaves and arrives back at school at 15:30hrs. (1) How long did the coach stop for? (2) What was the average speed on the return journey?

(1) From the distance-time graph above you can see it was stationary from 1300 – 1400hrs, which is 1hr

(Between these time intervals no further distance is covered, so it is stationary – see the vertical axis at 30 miles)

(2) The return journey starts at 1400hrs and ends at school at 1530hrs = 1.5 hrs.

Since **Speed** = $\frac{Distance}{Time}$, this means speed = 30÷1.5 = 20 mph

You might find the following conversions useful to go through

(Typically the Numerical reasoning test questions give you the conversion formula in the relevant questions)

1 km = 5/8 mile

1 mile =8/5 km

1kg =2.2 lb (approximately)

1 gallon =4.5 litres (approximately)

1 inch = 2.54 cm (approximately)

Chapter 7: Data Interpretation

Mean, Median, Mode and Range

First consider the different types of 'averages'.

That is Mean, Median, Mode and Range (You can try to remember these as: MMMR)

Mean: The sum of the numbers in a data set divided by the number of values in the
Set

Median: The middle number of a data set when listed in order

Mode: The most frequently occurring number or numbers in a data set

Range: The difference between the highest and the smallest numbers in a data set

Example 1:
Find the mean value of the following data set:
2, 7, 1, 1, 7, 8, 9

Method: Find the sum first
2 + 7 + 1 + 1 + 7 + 8 + 9 = 35
Now divide this total by 7, since this is the total number of numbers
So, 35/7 = 5
Hence, the mean value of this data set is 5

Example 2:
Find the median of 3, 7, 1, 8, and 6

Method: First re-order from smallest to biggest, re-writing the numbers we have: 1, 3, 6, 7, 8
Clearly the middle number is 6.
Hence, the median is 6

Example 3:
Find the median of 3, 6, 7, 1, 8 and 5

Method
First re-arrange to get 1, 3, 5, 6, 7, 8
Notice, in this case the middle number is between 5 & 6
So the median is (5 + 6)/2 = 5.5

Example 4:
Find the Range of the data set 3, 5, 7, 1, 8, and 11

Method: Find the difference between the biggest and smallest numbers
So the Range = 11 − 1 = 10

Example 5:
Find the Mode of the following numbers:
1, 4, 4, 4, 7, 8, 9, 9, 11, 12

Method: Find the most frequently occurring number. The most frequently occurring number is 4.
Hence the Mode is 4

Example 6:
Find the mode of 1, 3, 3, 3, 3 5, 5, 5, 5, 8, 8, 9

Method: As before find the most frequently occurring number(s).
Clearly there are two modes here. Both '3' and '5' occur most frequently, the same number of times, so we say this is a bi-modal distribution. That is, a distribution with two modes, namely 3 and 5

Pie Charts

When data is represented in a circle this is called a pie chart. Basically you need to remember that a full circle or 360 degrees represents all the data (or 100% of the data). Half a circle or 180 degrees represents half the data (or 50% of the data), and similarly 25% of the data is represented by 90 degrees or a quarter of a circle. Essentially, each sector or slice of the pie chart shows the proportion of the total data in that category.

Example 1:

The pie chart below shows the percentage of applicants who got different grades in a psychometric aptitude test when applying for a job in a particular company. The requirement to be short listed for a second interview was to pass with high marks. If 140 applicants took this test how many of them were short listed?

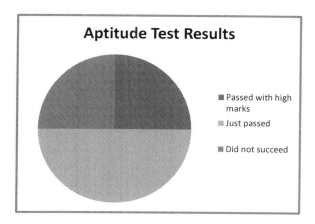

Method: As illustrated the results in this aptitude test for this particular company show that 25% got the required 'high marks' to be short listed for a second interview. Since a quarter of a circle corresponds to 25%. This means a quarter of the 140 applicants attained this which corresponds to 35 people.

<u>**Example 2:**</u>

The destination of 120 pupils who leave year 11 in School B in 2012 is represented in the pie chart below. The numbers outside the sectors represent the number of pupils

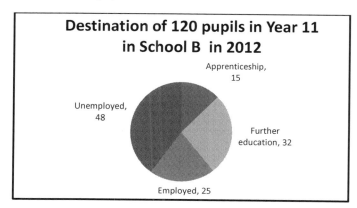

(1) What is the percentage of pupils who are unemployed?

Method:

The number of pupils out of 120 that are unemployed is 48. So the percentage of pupils who are unemployed is $\frac{48}{120} \times 100 = \frac{4800}{120} = \frac{480}{12} = 40\%$

(2) What fraction of pupils go on to Further Education?

Method:

The fraction of pupils that go on to further education is $\frac{32}{120} = \frac{8}{30} = \frac{4}{15}$, the fraction representing this in its simplest form is $\frac{4}{15}$

(3) What percentage of pupils is either employed or in apprenticeships? Give your answer to one decimal place?

Method:

Total number of pupils who are either in employment or apprenticeships = 25+15 =40, hence the percentage is $\frac{40}{120} \times 100 = \frac{4}{12} \times 100 = \frac{1}{3} \times 100 = 33.3\%$

Bar charts

Bar charts can be represented in columns or as horizontal bars. They can be either simple bar charts that show frequencies associated with data values or they can be multiple bar charts to allow for comparisons between data sets as shown below. The examples below illustrate some of the ways bar charts can be used to represent data.

Example 1: In a cosmetics shop the number of items that were sold for four top brands over a one month period were recorded as shown in the bar chart below.

(1) Which brand had the highest sales? **You can see from the column bar chart below that Brand D had the highest sales as 40 items of this brand were sold during one month, which is higher than any other brand**

(2) What was the proportion of sales for Brand D compared to the total? Give your answer as a fraction in its lowest terms. **The number of Brand A items sold were 20, Brand B were 35 and Brand C were 25 and as we saw earlier 40 items of Brand D were sold. This means the total number of cosmetic items**

sold during this one month period = 120. Since 40 items belonged to Brand D, compared to the total this is $\frac{40}{120}$ which simplifies to $\frac{1}{3}$

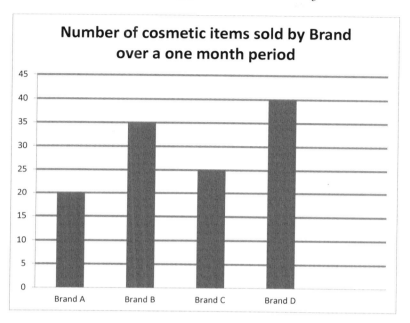

Example 2: The bar chart below shows the amount of time in hours John, Bob and Bill spend surfing the web at weekends. What is the mean time per boy that is spent Surfing the web at the weekend?

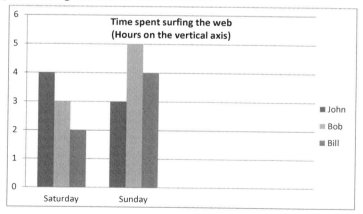

Method: John spends 4 hours on Saturday and 3 hours on a Sunday: a total of 7 hours. Bob spends a total of 3 hours on Saturday and 5 hours on Sunday: a total of 8 hours

Similarly, Bill spends a total of 2 + 4 = 6 hours on a weekend

Total time spent surfing between the 3 boys on a week end is 7+ 8 + 6 =21hours

Hence the mean time spent per boy is 21 ÷ 3 =7 hours

Example 3: Horizontal Bar Chart

In an on-line company the percentage of employees in 4 key departments is shown below. (1) If there are 560 employees altogether, how many are in the On-line marketing department? (2) How many more employees are there in On-line marketing compared to Customer Service department?

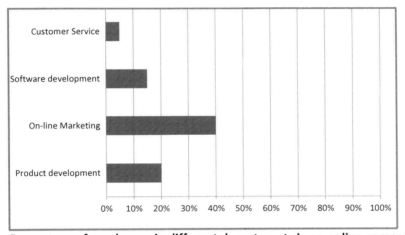

Percentage of employees in different departments in an online company

Method:

(1) From the bar chart you can see that 40% of the employees are in on-line marketing. Since there are 560 employees altogether, this means 40% of 560 = 224 employees (10% of 560 =56, hence 40% = 4×56 = 4×50 + 4×6 = 200 + 24 = 224)

(2) 5% of employees are in customer service. Since there are 560 employees altogether, 10% = 56 and 5% =28 employees. We know from the previous question that there are 224 employees in On-line marketing. 224 – 28 = 196 employees. This means there are 196 more employees in the On-line marketing department compared to the Customers Service Department.

Example 4:

This composite bar chart below shows the percentage of pupils in a particular school who take and do not take additional lessons in music and maths respectively. What is the proportion of pupils who take extra music lessons? Give your answer as a fraction in its lowest terms.

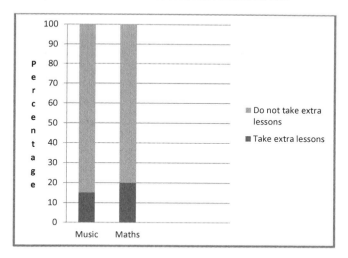

Method: The proportion of pupils who take extra music lessons is 15%. This is $\frac{15}{100}$ which simplifies to $\frac{3}{20}$. Hence $\frac{3}{20}$ of the pupils take extra lessons in music.

Scatter Graphs

Scatter graphs or diagrams are used to show the type of relationship between two variables, for example height and weight, maths and physics scores, reading scores and IQ and so on. It also gives information on the type of correlation between the two variables.

Positive Correlation

This means when the value of one variable increases so does the value of the other one as shown in the example below.

A certain number of pupils' test marks in maths and physics are plotted. (The straight line drawn is called the line of best fit.) . You can see in this case there is a positive correlation between Maths marks and Physics marks.

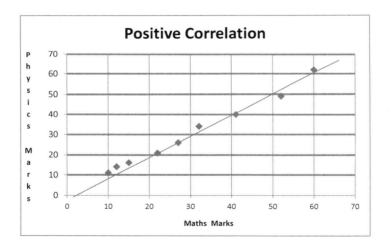

(1) How many pupils get more than 45 marks both in Maths and Physics?

Answer: 2 pupils get above 45 marks in both these subjects.

Method: look at the horizontal and vertical axis and draw an imaginary line at 45. Above 45 marks in both subjects you can see the record of two pupils.

(2) How many pupils get less than 20 marks in both Maths and Physics?

Answer: 3 pupils get less than 20 marks (using similar reasoning to the first answer)

Negative Correlation

This means that as one variable decreases in value the other one increases.

Example of Negative correlation:

This time some pupils' scores in Maths were plotted with their scores in History. It appears that in this particular case there was a negative correlation between Maths and History scores as shown below.

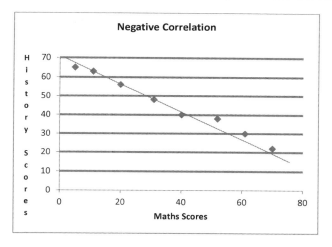

Another example of a negative correlation is the one between the price of a car and its age. As a car gets older its price is generally lower.

Zero Correlation

This is when there is no relationship between the two variables. The points are scattered all over the place so that we cannot really draw a line of best fit. For example consider the relationship between Science and English marks shown below in this particular example

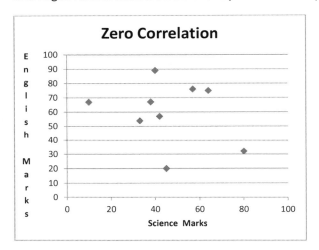

(1) In the example above what was the approximate mark in Science for the pupil who scored 20 marks in English?

Answer: 45 is the approximate mark in Science

Method: From the vertical axis, go along the horizontal line at 20 marks, this corresponds to approximately 45 marks in Science

It is worth remembering that we can have a weak positive correlation or a weak negative correlation. For example the percentage of men with grey hair is only weakly correlated with increasing age!

An example of scatter graph that shows a weak positive correlation, for example between Geography marks and History marks

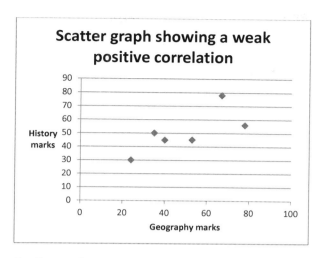

Scatter graph showing a weak positive correlation

Finally, just for interest it is worth remembering the difference between correlation and causation. For example the incidence of heart attacks is correlated with high total cholesterol, but it is worth noting that many people with high cholesterol do not have a heart attack. In fact, the incidence of heart attacks is correlated with total cholesterol, LDL, triglycerides, obesity, body mass index and genetic factors. In other words, in this case the incidence of heart disease is multifactorial (has many factors that are responsible) and to draw a causal link from one factor may be erroneous. Another interesting and controversial issue is that more vaccinations have resulted in a higher incidence of autism! Unfortunately, as vaccination rates went up in the USA so did the rates of autism. This led some people to falsely attribute vaccinations as the cause of autism. Autism has gone up for other reasons, more awareness leading to more diagnostic cases, genetic factors which we were not previously aware of and so on. Often there are other 'variables' involved. Unfortunately, journalists and sometimes even scientists jump to 'causal' conclusions. In higher level statistics there are methodologies of significance testing which help ascertain whether a correlation is likely to be 'causal' or whether there could be other factors at play.

Line graph

A line graph is a way to represent two sets of related data. **It is often used to show trends**

Example 1: The data below shows the percentage of candidates who had 'A' level mathematics who were short-listed for the first interview when applying to a consultancy company. This data is shown in the table below. However, the same data can be shown as a line graph that follows.

Year	2005	2006	2007	2008	2009	2010
% of candidates with 'A' level Maths	26%	35%	45%	37%	48%	32%

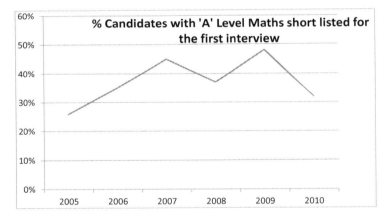

What was the change in percentage points for candidates that were short-listed between 2008 and 2010?

Method: You can see from the table as well as the graph that the success rate actually dropped from   (approx.) 37% to (approx) 32%. That is decreased by 5% points.

Example 2: The sales of Company A and Company B are plotted in a line graph from 2001 to 2006. If 850 employees worked for Company A and 800 employees worked for Company B in 2006. What was the sales per employee for Company B in 2006?

Sales of Company A and Company B from 2001 - 2006 in £ million

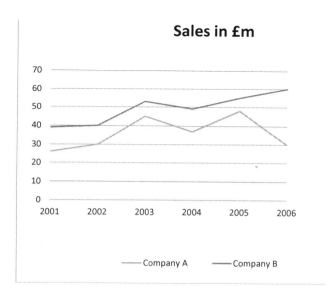

Method: From the line graph it can be seen that in 2006, Company B had a sales of £60 million. If 800 employees worked for this company, then clearly the sales per employee was £60,000,000 ÷ 800 = 600,000÷8 = 300,000÷4 =150,000÷2 = £75000. Hence, the sales per employee in Company B in 2006 was £75000.

Chapter 8   Probability

Probability is defined as the likelihood of an event happening. Probability lies between 0 and 1.

A probability of 0 means that an event will definitely not happen or it is impossible to happen. Likewise a probability of 1 means is certain to happen. Probability is usually expressed as a fraction, a decimal or a percentage.

Consider two simple cases: There are 4 blue balls in a bag. You take out a ball at random. (1) What is the probability that the ball you pick is red? (2) What is the probability that the ball you pick is blue? Although this is a trivial example you can see that in question (1) it is impossible to pick red ball since all the 4 balls in the bag are blue. Hence the probability of picking up a red ball is 0. Similarly, in question (2) the probability that you pick a blue ball is 1. That is you are certain to pick a blue ball, since all the four balls are blue.

Many events of course happen with a probability between 0 & 1. For example a probability of 0.8 would indicate a fairly high chance of an event happening, whereas a probability of 0.2 would imply a low probability of an event happening. The probability of an event happening is defined as:

$$\frac{number\ of\ ways\ in\ which\ the\ event\ can\ happen}{total\ number\ of\ outcomes}$$

Also note that the probability of an event **not happening** is **1 – the probability of an event happening**

Notation used: P(A) means probability of event A happening. Hence probability of event A not happening would be 1 – P(A).

Typical examples:

Example 1:

There are 5 red, 6 green and 7 blue beads in a bag.

(1) You pick a bead at random from the bag. What is the probability of picking a red bead? Answer $P(R) = \frac{5}{18}$ (Reason: there are 18 beads altogether, and 5 of them are red, so the chance or probability of picking a red bead is 5 in 18 or $\frac{5}{18}$)

---

(2) What is the probability of picking a green or blue bead? Answer
$$P(G \ or \ B) = \frac{13}{18}$$

Reason: there are 18 beads altogether, and the number of green and blue beads combined total 13. Hence the probability of picking a green or blue bead is 13 in 18 or $\frac{13}{18}$.

(3) What is the probability of not picking a green bead? Answer: P(not G) = 1 – P(G) = 1 - $\frac{6}{18}$ = $\frac{12}{18}$

A simpler way of doing the same problem is to say that since there are 18 beads altogether and 6 of them are green, then this means that 12 are not green, hence the probability of not picking up a green bead is 12 in 18 that is $\frac{12}{18}$. You could of course simplify $\frac{12}{18}$ to $\frac{2}{3}$ (dividing both the top number 12 and bottom number 18, by 6)

Relative Frequencies:

When you do not know the probability exactly you can use an experimental method of relative frequencies to assess an **estimate** of the probability. Let's say you are not sure whether a die is fair or biased. You test it out by throwing it 200 times and get the number 6, fifty times.

Relative frequency of an event is defined as

$$= \frac{Number \ of \ times \ the \ event \ happened}{Total \ number \ of \ trials}$$

In this example, using the formula above the relative frequency $= \frac{50}{200} = \frac{5}{20} = \frac{1}{4} = $ 0.25, it seems that the die is biased as we would expect the number 6 to occur roughly $\frac{1}{6} \times 200$ times which is around 33 times! (Just for interest to be absolutely sure that the result wasn't just a coincidence we may need to repeat the experiment again with a bigger sample and also do something called 'significance' testing to make sure that the die is really biased)

Expected Number

Example 1: If a fair die is thrown 660 times approximately how many threes are we likely to get?

The probability of getting any number when a fair die is thrown is $\frac{1}{6}$. The expected number of threes = P(3) × 660 = $\frac{1}{6}$ x 660 = 110. We would therefore expect the number three to occur 110 times.

Example 2: In a certain company, the probability of passing a numerical skills test by any individual is 0.45. If 100 candidates take this test over a year, how many individuals do you expect to pass this test?

Method: 100 × 0.45 = 45. So we would expect 45 candidates to pass this test.

Multiplication law in probability

When you have independent events (that is the outcome of one is not affected by the outcome of the other) then to find the probability of say event A and event B happening we simply multiply the probabilities of A and B together.

Example 1: What is the probability that we will get two sixes when a die is rolled two times?

Method: Probability that we get '6' followed by '6' = $\frac{1}{6} \times \frac{1}{6} = \frac{1}{36}$

Example 2: A fair coin is flipped three times. What is the probability it will turn up 'heads' on all three occasions? Give your answer to 2 decimal places.

Method: Probability that it turns up 'heads' **and** 'heads' **and** 'heads' = $\frac{1}{2} \times \frac{1}{2} \times \frac{1}{2} = \frac{1}{8}$ =0.125 or 0.13 to 2 decimal places. Or you could have calculated it another way i.e. 0.5×0.5×0.5 = 0.25×0.5 =0.125 and then give your answer to two decimal places 0.13 as required.

Example 3: If a fair die is thrown twice what is the probability of getting a 'six' followed by 'not a six'. Give your answer as a fraction.

Method: P(getting a six) = $\frac{1}{6}$, so the probability of 'not getting a six' = 1 - $\frac{1}{6}$ = $\frac{5}{6}$. Hence the probability that you get a 'six' followed by 'not a six' = $\frac{1}{6} \times \frac{5}{6} = \frac{5}{36}$

Addition law in probability: When two or more events are mutually exclusive (i.e. they cannot occur together), then the probability of A **or** B **or** C happening is simply found by adding the respective probabilities. That is p(A) + p(B) + p(C).

Example 1: there are 6 blue beads, 8 green beads and 15 black beads in a bag. What is the probability of picking either a green or a black bead?

Method: altogether there are 29 beads. Probability of picking a green bead $=\frac{8}{29}$, similarly the probability of picking a black bead $=\frac{15}{29}$. Hence the probability of picking either a green or black bead is found by adding the two probabilities together. P(Green or Black) $=\frac{8}{29}+\frac{15}{29}=\frac{23}{29}$

Example 2: A pack of 52 cards is shuffled. What is the probability of picking an ace or a king or a Queen? Give your answer in its simplest form?

Method: There are 52 cards altogether. There are 4 aces, 4 kings and 4 Queens in a pack of cards. Hence the probability of picking an Ace 'or' a King 'or' a Queen $=\frac{4}{52}+\frac{4}{52}+\frac{4}{52}=\frac{12}{52}=\frac{6}{26}=\frac{3}{13}$

Problems 'with' and 'without' replacement

Example 1: There are 3 red marbles and 7 blue marbles in a bag. A marble is picked at random. It is put back in the bag and another marble is picked at random. What is the probability of picking two red marbles consecutively?

You can see that this is a fairly straight forward problem. There are 10 marbles altogether and 3 of them are red. The probability of picking a red marble the first time is thus $\frac{3}{10}$. Since the marble that you pick the first time is now put back you have the same situation as before, so the probability of picking a red marble the second time is also $\frac{3}{10}$. Hence, the probability of picking a red marble followed by another red marble is $\frac{3}{10}\times\frac{3}{10}=\frac{9}{100}$

Example 2: Now consider this, let's say there are still 3 red marbles and 7 blue marbles in a bag. You pick up one but don't put it back in the bag. If you pick up a red marble the first time, then there are now only 2 red marbles and 7 blue marbles left. The probability of picking up a red marble the first time is still $\frac{3}{10}$ but the probability of picking up a red marble the second time is now $\frac{2}{9}$. (since there are now 9 marbles in total of which 2 are red). Hence the probability of picking up 2 red balls consecutively on this occasion is $\frac{3}{10}\times\frac{2}{9}=\frac{6}{90}$ or $\frac{1}{15}$ writing the fraction in its simplest form!

Example 3: What is the probability of picking two aces consecutively from a shuffled pack of cards?

You can see that the first time you pick a card up there are 4 aces and 52 cards, but once you pick up an ace there are now only 3 aces left and 51 cards altogether. Hence the probability of picking up two aces consecutively is $\frac{4}{52}$ x $\frac{3}{51}$. This can be simplified by cancelling down the two fractions. The first fraction $\frac{4}{52}$ can be simplified to $\frac{1}{13}$ and the second fraction $\frac{3}{51}$ can be simplified to $\frac{1}{17}$. Hence , $\frac{4}{52}$ x $\frac{3}{51}$ can be re-written as $\frac{1}{13}$ x $\frac{1}{17}$ = $\frac{1}{221}$

Tree diagrams are another way of solving probability problems showing two or more events.

Example: In year7 the probability that a pupil does his homework is $\frac{3}{8}$ and the probability that a pupil comes late to class is $\frac{5}{6}$. These two events are independent. Draw a tree diagram and find the probability that a given pupil does the homework and is late for class.

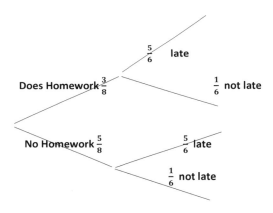

Method: To do this using the tree diagram we simply follow the branch 'does homework' **and** 'late' As you can see the probability in this case is $\frac{3}{8}$ × $\frac{5}{6}$ = $\frac{15}{48}$ = $\frac{5}{16}$ in its simplest form

Summary:

(1) Probability lies between 0 and 1 and is usually expressed as a decimal, a fraction or a percentage. The probability of an event can never exceed 1.

(2) When events are independent, to find the probability of A <u>and</u> B occurring together we <u>multiply</u> the probabilities of the respective events. Remember the word <u>'and' is associated with 'x' or multiplication</u>.

(3) When events are mutually exclusive the probability of A <u>or</u> B <u>or</u> C happening is found by <u>adding</u> the individual probabilities. Remember the word <u>'or' is associated with '+' or addition</u>.

(4) When working out probabilities consider whether it is 'with' or 'without' replacement

(5) You can generate tree diagrams or sample space diagrams to visualize probabilities and outcomes if it helps you.

Chapter 9   Introduction to Algebra

In algebra we often use letters instead of numbers. There are some basic conventions and rules of algebra that you should be familiar with to progress in this subject.

If you see	We mean
$x = y$	x equals y
$x > y$	x is greater than y
$x < y$	x is less than y
$x \geq y$	x is greater than or equal to y
$x \leq y$	x is less than or equal to y
$x + y$	the sum of x and y
$x - y$	subtract y from x
xy	x times y
x/y	x divided by y
$x \div y$	x divided by y
x^n	x to the power n
$x(x + y)$	x times the sum of x + y

Also note that:

$x(x + y) = x^2 + xy$

$x^2(x + x^2 + y) = x^3 + x^4 + x^2 y$

In general, $a \times a \times a \times a \ \text{.......(n times)} = a^n$

Also note an important symbol you will come across quite often in maths.

$\Longrightarrow$ This arrow means 'It implies that'

For Example if **something plus 3 = 5** then $\Longrightarrow$ that **something = 2!**

You also need to know these algebraic rules for the multiplication and division of positive and negative numbers.

Multiplying positive and negative numbers.

(+) × (+) = +   (a plus number times a plus number gives us a plus number)

(+) × (−) = −   (a plus number times a minus number gives us a minus number)

(−) × (+) = −   (a minus number times a plus number gives us a minus number)

(−) × (−) = +   (a minus number times a minus number gives us a plus number)

Dividing positive and negative numbers.

(+) ÷ (+)= + (a plus number divided by a plus number gives us a plus number)

(+) ÷ (−)= − (a plus number divided by a minus number gives us a minus number)

(−) ÷ (+) = − (a minus number divided by a plus number gives us a minus number)

(−) ÷ (−) = +   (a minus number times a minus number gives us a plus number)

Summary: <u>For both multiplication and division, like signs gives us a plus sign and unlike signs gives a minus sign</u>

Also when adding and subtracting it is worth knowing that:

When you add two minus numbers you get a bigger minus number.

<u>Example 1:</u> −4 − 6 = −10

When you add a plus number and a minus number you get the sign corresponding to the bigger number as shown below:

<u>Example 2:</u> +6 − 9 =−3, whereas, −6+9 =3

When you subtract a minus from a plus or minus number you need to note the results as shown below:

<u>Example 3</u>: 6 − (− 3) we get 6+3 =9 (since −(−3) =+3)

Example 4: $7 - (+3)$ we get $7 - 3 = 4$ (since $- (+3) = -3$)

In this case note that $- (-) = +$. Also, $+(-) = -$ and $- (+) = -$.

Finally you need to know the rules concerning the operation of numbers and one more symbol:

By operations we mean working out powers of numbers, multiplication, division, addition and subtraction. These operations need to be performed in the right order. Failing to do this might give you wrong results.

The rule taught traditionally is that of **BIDMAS.**

The **BIDMAS** rule is as follows:

(5) Always work out the **B**racket(s) first
(6) Then work out the Indices of a number (squares, cubes, square roots and so on)
(7) Now **M**ultiply and **D**ivide
(8) Finally do the **A**ddition and **S**ubtraction.

Example 1: Work out $2(4+6) - 4$

Work out the bracket first then times by 2 to get $2 \times 10 = 20$. Finally take away 4 to get 16

So $2(4+6) - 4 = 16$

Example 2: $3 \times 4^2 + 13(7 - 2)$

The first part is 3×16 (we square before multiplying)

The second part is 13×5 (we do the brackets and then multiply)

The first part is thus 48 and the second part 65. Adding these two parts together we have 113.

So, $3 \times 4^2 + 13(7 - 2) = 113$

Simplifying algebraic expressions.

(This is a process where we collect like terms as shown in the examples below)

Example 1: Simplify 3x + 4x + 5x

Method: We simple add up all the x's.

Hence we get 3x+4x+5x = 12x

Example2: Simplify 3x +4x +3y +5y

Method: Add up all the like terms.

So we get 3x + 4x + 3y + 5y = 7x +8y

(Notice we add up all the x's and all the y's)

Example 3: Simplify 3m + 4y +2m − 3y

Method: as before, we add and subtract like terms.

Now 3m+2m =5m and 4y-3y =1y or just y.

So we can write 3m +4y +2m −3y = 5m + y.

Example 4: Simplify 3m +3n −2(2m+4n)

Method: Using the rules we learnt earlier, we have:

3m +3n −2(2m+4n)= 3m +3n −4m − 8n

Notice that we get −4m −8n since −2x2m =−4m and −2x4n = −-8n

Finally 3m +3n −4m −8n = −m −5n

Example 5: Simplify $3m^2 +4y^3 +4m^2 - 5y^3$

Method: We add and subtract like terms.

Now $3m^2 +4m^2 = 7m^2$ and $4y^3 - 5y^3 = - y^3$

Hence, $3m^2 +4y^3 +4m^2 - 5y^3 = 7m^2 - y^3$

Multiplying out brackets.

Example 1: Expand 3(2x +5)

Method: we multiply 3 by each term in the bracket. So we get $3 \times 2x + 3 \times 5$ which gives us $6x + 15$.

Example 2: Expand and simplify $3(2x +5) +4(2x+7)$

Method: Multiply 3 by each term in the first bracket then 4 by each term in the second bracket. The final step is to simplify by collecting up the like terms.

$3(2x+5) +4(2x+7) =6x+15+8x+28 =14x + 43$

Notice the last step is simply adding $6x + 8x$ and then $15+28$.

Example 3: Work out $5(2x -5) - 6(3x - 4)$

This gives us $10x - 25 - 18x +24 = -8x - 1$

Example 4: Work out $(2x+3)(2x+4)$

When we have to multiply out two brackets we have to multiply each term in the first bracket by each term in the second bracket. We then simplify the resulting expression as before. An easy way to multiply out two brackets is to use the grid method as shown below:

First put each of the terms of each bracket on the outside grid as shown

×	2x	+3
2x		
+4		

Step2: Multiply each outside term together. So that for example $2x \times 2x = 4x^2$. The other results are shown inside the grid.

X	2x	+ 3
2x	$4x^2$	+ 6x
+ 4	8x	+12

After multiplying out the terms, the answer is found by adding all the terms inside the grid and simplifying the resulting expression.

So we have, $4x^2 + 6x + 8x + 12$ (These are all the terms inside the grid)

Finally, $4x^2 + 6x + 8x + 12 = 4x^2 + 14x + 12$

Another example will help consolidate the process:

Multiply out $(2x - 3)(3x + 2)$

Put the terms of each bracket on the outside of the grid as shown

X	2x	−3
3x	$6x^2$	− 9x
+ 2	4x	− 6

Collecting up all the terms inside the grid we have:

$6x^2 - 9x + 4x - 6$

Now simplifying this gives us, $6x^2 - 5x - 6$

Another way of expanding brackets

Example 1: Expand $(x + 3)(x + 2)$

(Multiply the first term of the first bracket by the second bracket and then multiply the second term of the first bracket by the second bracket. Finally simplify the expression.)

So $(x + 3)(x + 2) = x(x + 2) + 3(x + 2) = x^2 + 2x + 3x + 6 = x^2 + 5x + 6$

Example 2: Expand $(2x - 1)(x - 2)$

This equals $2x(x - 2) - 1(x - 2) = 2x^2 - 4x - x + 2 = 2x^2 - 5x + 2$

Example 3: Expand $(y^2 + x)(y - x^2)$

$= y^2(y - x^2) + x(y - x^2) = y^3 - y^2x^2 + xy - x^3$

Chapter 10   Solving equations

Simple Equations

Consider the following English statements and their mathematical equivalent:

English Statements	Algebra
Something plus five equals ten	$x + 5 = 10$
Something times two, plus five equals eleven	$2x + 5 = 11$
Something times three, minus five equals thirteen	$3x - 5 = 13$
Something divided by two equals three	$x/2 = 3$

Now consider solving these equations using a common sense approach.

Example 1: Something plus five equals ten. What is 'something'?

Clearly we need to add five to five to get ten. So 'something' in this case equals five.

Solving this by algebra can be very similar. As we saw, we can re-write the English statement above in algebra as follows:

$x + 5 = 10$ (notice, we are representing 'something' by x)

Now, if $x + 5 = 10$ clearly x (which represents 'something') is equal to 5.

So, x = 5

Example 2: 'Something' times two plus five equals eleven. Find the 'something'.

We know that 'something' times two plus five equals eleven.

So the two times 'something' must equal 6. In which case 'something' must be 3.

Now consider the algebraic equivalent.

$2x + 5 = 11$

This means $2x = 6$

Which means $x = 3$

Now consider a more formal method.

Imagine an equation like a balance. Whatever you do to one side you must do to the other.

Example 3: Solve the equation $x + 5 = 10$

Subtract 5 from both sides

So, $x = 5$

However, we can also use the method of taking inverses.

The rules are: When something is added to the x-term subtract, when something is subtracted from the x-term then add. When x, is multiplied, by a number we divide. Finally, when the x-term, is divided, by a number we multiply.

Example 4: Solve the equation $2x + 5 = 11$

Subtract 5 from both sides (that is, take the inverse of +5)

So, $2x = 6$

Now divide both sides by 2(that is, take the inverse of X2)

So, $x = 3$.

Example 5: Solve the equation $3x - 5 = 13$

This time add 5 to both sides giving:

$3x = 18$

Now divide both sides by 3 which gives, $x = 6$

Example 6: Solve the equation $5x - 1 = 2x + 8$

First add 1 to both sides, which gives:

$5x = 2x + 9$

Now subtract 2x from both sides to give $3x = 9$

Finally divide both sides by 3 to get $x = 3$.

(Notice each step simplifies the equation further)

Example 7: Solve the equation $5(2x + 1) = 4(2x + 1)$

To solve this first multiply out the bracket which gives:

$10x + 5 = 8x + 4$

(Multiply each term outside the bracket by each term inside the bracket)

Now subtract 5 from both sides, which gives:

$10x = 8x - 1$

Now subtract 8x from both sides, which gives:

$2x = -1$

Finally, divide both sides by 2 to get $x = -1/2$ or -0.5

Example 8: Solve the equation $\frac{2x}{3} + 5 = 7$

We can simplify this to $\frac{2x}{3} = 2$ (by subtracting 5 from both sides)

Now multiply both sides by 3 to get the expression below:

$2x = 6$,   So $x = 3$

Summary:

The key point to remember is that you reverse the operation to eliminate a number from one side. This is called the method of taking inverses. So if $x + 5 = 10$ then to get rid of the 5 from the left hand side we subtract 5 from both sides. Similarly if, $3x = 18$ then divide both sides by 3 to find x.

Chapter 11   Geometry

Reminder of angles, triangles, parallel lines, common shapes & polygons

(1) Angles on a straight line add up to 180 degrees

(2) The sum of the angles in a triangle add up to 180 degrees

(3) Right angled triangle   **(4)** Equilateral triangle

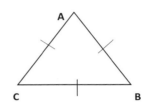

Right- angled triangle   **Equilateral Triangle**

Angle ACB = 90 degrees   **All sides and angles are equal**

                                              Each angle = 60 degrees

(5) Isosceles triangle

Isosceles triangle

Base angles are equal

Two sides are equal

(6) Exterior angle of a triangle

Exterior angle ABD = the sum of the opposite angles (angle BAC plus angle ACB)

Parallel lines

angle m = angle n

(corresponding angles)

angle x = angle y (alternate angles)

a + b = 180 degrees

Quadrilateral – 4 sided shape

The sum of the angles of a quadrilateral add up to 360 degrees

Square

Rectangle

Parallelogram

Trapezium

Rhombus (a squashed square)

Kite

Regular Polygons

A regular polygon is where all the sides and angles are equal.

Consider these typical regular polygons:

Regular 3 –sided polygon

Equilateral triangle (all sides equal)

Regular 4 – sided polygon

Square

Regular Pentagon (5 sides)

Regular Hexagon (6 sides)

Regular Heptagon (7 sides)

Regular Octagon (8 sides)

Useful formulas for polygons that you should memorize:

Exterior angle = $\frac{360}{n}$

Interior angle = 180° - exterior angle = $180 - \frac{360}{n}$ which simplifies to $\frac{180n-360}{n}$
= $\frac{180(n-2)}{n}$

Angle based examples concerning triangles, parallelograms and polygons

Example 1: Find the interior angle x and the exterior angle y in the triangle below:

Method: 2x + x + 60 = 180 (interior angles of a triangle add up to 180°). This means 3x + 60 = 180, simplifying this we get 3x = 120. This means x =40°

To find y we can use the fact that x + y =180. This means 40 + y = 180, hence y =140°. So x = 40° and y = 140°

Example 2:

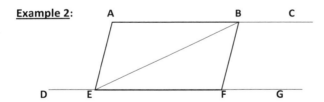

ABFE is a parallelogram. Angle ABE = 30° and angle BFG = 70°

Calculate angle AEB.

Method: Clearly angle BFE = 180 – 70 = 110° Also angle BEF = 30° (Alternate angle to angle ABE).

Now consider triangle BFE. Since we know two angles (angle BEF and angle BFE) we can work out the value of angle EBF. Angle EBF = 180 – (110 + 30) = 40°

Finally, angle AEB = angle EBF (alternate angles)

So angle AEB = 40∘

Example 3:

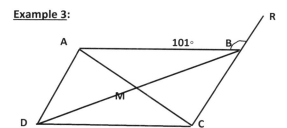

ABCD is a parallelogram. Angle ABR =101∘ and angle BAC = 30∘. You are also given that angle DMC =110∘. Work out the size of the angle ADM.

Method: Angle AMB =110∘ (Since angles DMC and AMC are opposite angles)

Consider triangle ABM

Angle ABM = 180 – (30 + 110) = 40∘ (Angles in triangle =180∘)

Now since CBR is a straight line then angle MBC + angle ABM + angle ABR = 180∘. This means that angle MBC + 40∘ +101∘ =180∘, so angle MBC = 180 – 141 that is angle MBC = 39∘

Finally since angle ADM and angle MBC are alternate angles this means angle ADM also = 39∘

Example 4: Find the interior and exterior angle of a regular octagon.

Using the formula above the interior angle is $\frac{180(n-2)}{n} = \frac{180(8-2)}{8} = \frac{180\times6}{8} = \frac{90\times6}{4}$
$= \frac{90\times3}{2} = \frac{45\times3}{1} = 135∘$

Hence the exterior angle is 180 – 135 = 45∘

Chapter 12   Areas and Volumes of common shapes

Perimeters, Areas and Volumes of common shapes

Consider the shapes below:

(1) Rectangle

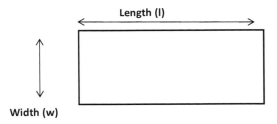

Area of a rectangle = Length X Width or l × w

Perimeter of a rectangle = 2l + 2w (distance around the rectangle)

Note: Area is measured in units squared, e.g. cm^2 or m^2 and perimeter (distance all round a shape) is measured in the appropriate units e.g. cm or m

(2) Triangle

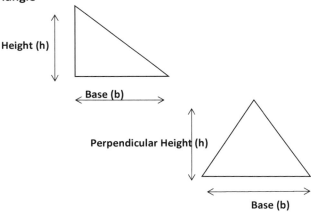

Area of a triangle =1/2 × base × height or $\frac{b \times h}{2}$ (The height is the perpendicular height relative to the base)

Area of a Trapezium

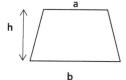

Area of a trapezium = (half the sum of the parallel sides × perpendicular height) = $\frac{(a+b)h}{2}$

Area of a circle is πr^2 (this means the value of π(pi) multiplied by radius squared)

Circumference of a circle (distance all the way round a circle) = 2πr or πd

2πr (2 × π × radius) **or** π × diameter

Note: Diameter of a circle = 2 × Radius

Approximate value of π = 3.142

Volume of a cuboid (or a box)

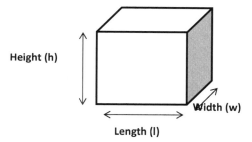

Volume of a cuboid is Height × Length × Width or V = h×l×w (units cubed e.g. cm^3 or m^3, etc)

Chapter 13   Some Useful Definitions and Reminders

Natural Numbers: are {1, 2, 3, 4, ...}

Whole Numbers: are {0, 1, 2, 3, ...}

Integers: These are whole numbers that include both positive and negative numbers including 0. So for example ....-5,-4,-3,-2, 0, 1, 2, 3, 4, ... are all integers.

Multiples: These are simply numbers in the multiplication tables.

For example the multiples of 6 are 6, 12, 18, 24, 30, ...

Factors: A factor is a number that divides exactly into another number as for example, the number 2 in the case of even numbers.

3 is a factor of 9, as 3 goes exactly into 9. Other factors of 9 are 1 and 9.

15, has two factors other than 15 and 1. The two factors are 5 and 3, since both these numbers go exactly into 15. **Example:** Find all the factors of 21. The factors are: 1, 3, 7 and 21 (since all these numbers divide exactly into 21)

Prime numbers: A prime number is a natural number that can be divided only by itself and by 1 (without a remainder). For example, 11 can be divided only by 1 and by 11. Prime numbers are whole numbers greater than 1. So for example the first 10 prime numbers are: 2, 3, 5, 7, 11, 13, 17, 19, 23 and 29. **Be careful that an odd number is not necessarily a prime number.** For example **9 is not a prime number** as its factors are 1, 3 and 9 and **prime numbers should have only two factors, 1 and the number itself. Also, note that 2 is a prime number, the only even number that can be divided by 1 and itself!**

Prime Factors: Some numbers can be written as a product of prime factors.

Example1: Write 28 as a product of prime factors.

Dividing 28 by the first prime factor 2 we are left with 14. Dividing 14 again by the first prime factor 2, we get 7. Now we can no longer divide 7 by the first prime factor 2. The next possible prime factor for 7 is obviously 7. **Hence 28 can be written as 2×2×7 or $2^2 \times 7$**

Example 2: Write the number 300 as a product of prime factors.

Step1: Divide by 300 by 2 to get 150,

Step 2: Divide 150 by 2 to get 75

Step 3: Divide 75 by 3 to get 25, Step 4: Divide 25 by 5 to get 5

Step 4: Divide 5 by 5 to get 1. Hence, **300 = 2×2×3×5×5 or $2^2 \times 3 \times 5^2$**

Another method of finding prime factors: Break down the required number at the top by dividing by prime factors starting with the lowest prime factor as shown below:

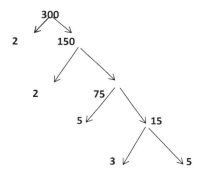

Hence the product of prime factors for **300 = 2×2×3×5×5 or $2^2 \times 3 \times 5^2$**

Lowest Common Multiple (LCM)

This is essentially the smallest number that will divide exactly by the numbers given. Consider the examples below:

Example 1: Find the LCM of 15 and 45

One method is to find the multiples of both numbers and identify the lowest common multiple as shown below:

Multiples of 15 = 15, 30, **45**, 60, 90, ……..

Multiples of 45 = **45**, 90, 135, 180, ……

Clearly **45** (the highlighted number above) is the smallest number that is divisible by 15 and 45.

Example 2: Find the LCM of 10 & 15

First find the multiples of each number:

Multiples of 10 = 10, 20, **30**, 40, 50, 60, 70,.....

Multiples of 15 = 15, **30,** 45, 60, ...

You can see that **30** is the lowest common multiple since it is divisible both by 10 & 15.

Highest Common Factor (HCF)

This is the biggest number that will divide exactly into all the numbers given

Example 1: Find the HCF of 15 & 45

Method: Find the factors of each number given and then identify the biggest number that will divide into both these numbers as shown below:

Factors of 15 ={1, 3, 5, **15**}, Factors of 45 ={1, 3, 5, 9, **15**, 45}

You can see that **15** is the **highest common factor** which divides into **both** 15 and 45 exactly.

Example 2: Find the HCF of 8 and 32.

First find the factors of each number given

Factors of 8 ={1, 2, 4, **8**}, Factors of 32 = {1, 2, 4, **8**, 16, 32}

You can see that the number 8 is the highest **common** factor which divides into 8 and 32 exactly.

Square numbers and square roots

Squaring a number is simply multiplying a number by itself.

So 4^2 means $4 \times 4 = 16$, 12^2 means $12 \times 12 = 144$ and so on.

The square root is written like this $\sqrt{}$ and means finding a number which when multiplied by itself gives you the number inside the square root.

Example1: Find $\sqrt{16}$. The answer is clearly 4. Since 4×4 =16

Let us consider some other square roots.

$\sqrt{49} = 7$, $\sqrt{121} = 11$, $\sqrt{100} = 10$, $\sqrt{225} = 15$,

$\sqrt{256} = 16$, $\sqrt{324} = 18$

Cubes and cubic roots

Cubing a number is simply multiplying the number by itself three consecutive times. A cube of a number is written as x^3, where x is the number.

So, for example, 5^3 means $5 \times 5 \times 5 = 25 \times 5 = 125$

Similarly, $6^3 = 6 \times 6 \times 6 = 216$, $7^3 = 7 \times 7 \times 7 = 343$, $9^3 = 9 \times 9 \times 9 = 729$,

$10^3 = 10 \times 10 \times 10 = 1000$

Cube Roots

Cube roots are found by finding a number which when cubed gives you the number inside the cube root.

So for example the cube root of 125 is written as $\sqrt[3]{125}$

Also we know that 5X5X5 =125, so that $\sqrt[3]{125} = 5$

Practice Questions 1 (No calculators allowed)

(1) Work out 27 X 17

(2) Find 15% of £300

(3) What is 124 ÷ 100

(4) What is 327 ÷ 0.1

(5) Find $2\frac{3}{4}$ of 460

(6) If I travel 60km in 2.5 hours, what is my average speed?

(7) There are 21 employees in a small company. Three of them go on a special training course. What is the fraction of employees that do not go on this training course? Give your answer in its lowest terms.

(8) 2500 millilitres of liquid is divided into 20 containers. How many millilitres of liquid does each container have?

(9) A walking group walks 24 Km every week.

If 8km is approximately equal to 5 miles, estimate how many miles the weekly walk consist of?

(10) 18 people are asked to collect £3.50 each for a charity. All of them succeed. What is the total amount collected?

(11) A group activity consists of 16 tasks. Each task lasts 15 minutes. How many hours will this group activity last?

(12) A meeting begins at 10:50. There is a general introduction for 6 minutes, a power-point presentation for 18 minutes and finally a question and answer session for 26 minutes. When does the meeting end? Give your answer using the 24-hour clock.

(13) A company calculated that it had given bonuses to its junior and senior staff in the ratio of 1:3. There was a total of £68000 bonus given. Assuming there were 20 senior staff, how much did each member of the senior staff get?

(14) A teacher has to see 16 parents for 12 minutes each to discuss pupil progress. In addition there is a 25 minute break. How long does the parents' session last in hours and minutes?

(15) In a numerical reasoning test an applicant achieved 27 out of 45 marks. What was the percentage mark that the applicant received in this test?

Answers to Practice Questions 1

1. 27 X17 = 459

   Method 27X17 = 27X10 + 27X5 +27X2 =270 +135+54 = 459

2. 15% of £300 = £45

   Method: 10% =£30 & 5% = £15, Hence total = £45

3. 124 ÷ 100 = 1.24

4. 327 ÷ 0.1 =3270 (remember when dividing by 0.1, you are effectively dividing by one tenth)

5. $2\frac{3}{4}$ of 460 = 1265

   Method: double 460 + half of 460 + a quarter of 460 = 920 +230 +115 = 1265

6. Average Speed = 24km/hour

   Method: Speed = Distance÷Time = 60÷2.5 = 24

7. The number of employees that do not go on a training course is $\frac{6}{7}$

   Method: Number of employees that do not go on a training course is 18. Hence fraction of employees that do not go = $\frac{18}{21}$ which simplifies to $\frac{6}{7}$ (Divide the top and bottom numbers of $\frac{18}{21}$ by 3

8. Each container has 125ml of liquid

   Method: 2500 ÷ 20 =125

9. The weekly walk consists of 15miles. Method: Since 8km = 5miles then

   24 km =24X$\frac{5}{8}$ = 120÷ 8 = 60 ÷ 4 = 15

10. Total amount collected = £63

    Method: 18X3 + 0.5X18 =54 + 9 =£63

11. The group activity lasts for 4hours

    Method: 16X 15 =16X10 + 16X5 = 160 + 80 =240 minutes = 4hrs

12. Meeting ends at 11:40

    Method: 6+ 18 + 26 = 50 minutes. Add 50 mins to 10:50 to get 11:40

13. Each senior member gets £2550

Method: Total parts in ratio = 4, therefore each part = 68000/4
= £17000. Senior staff get 3X as much = £51000. Since there are 20
senior staff each member of the senior staff gets £2550

14. The parents' session lasts 3 hours and 37 minutes

Method: 16 X 12 +25 (min break) = 192 +25 = 217 minutes
Since 180 minutes = 3 hours, we are left with 37 minutes. Hence total
time taken = 3 hours 37 minutes

15. 60%

Method: The applicant received 27 marks out of 45

Hence the percentage mark was $\frac{27}{45}$ X 100 = 60%

Practice Questions 2 (Calculators allowed)

(1) An employee attends a course which is 81.5 miles away. She is allowed to claim travel expenses for the journey there and back at 40p per mile. How much is the employee allowed to claim?

(2) A school organizes a day trip to the local museum. There are 48 pupils altogether. There is requirement for one adult per 8 pupils. What is the total number of people on this trip?

(3) A food retailer decides to pay 1.5% of its profits as bonuses to its frontline staff. In 2010 the retailer made 22 million pounds of profit. Assuming the retailer had 250 front line staff, how much approximately did each member of the staff receive in bonuses?

(4) A young couple bought a one bedroom flat in London for £180,000 at the beginning of 2005. The prices increased by 2% per annum from 2005 to 2012. What was the value of the house at the end of 2012. Give your answer to the nearest whole number.

(5) A meeting ends at 1425. The meeting was in two parts, starting with a presentation that lasted 30 minutes and ending with a discussion lasting 20 minutes. When did the meeting start?

(6) The ratio of male to female workers in company A is 4:5. Assuming there are 945 employees altogether, how many of the employees are male?

(7) A book store orders 80 fast selling books at £2.99 each. They sell each book at £6.70. How much profit will they make if they manage to sell all the books?

(8) A firm has a fund raising day for an educational charity they support. On average each employee contributes £4.75 towards this charity. 340 employees contributed this amount. How much is collected in total?

(9) Employees have access to a lawn area for general relaxation. The lawn is rectangular with a circular pool in the grounds. The lawn is 8.5m long and 4.5m wide. The pool has a radius of 1m. What is the area of the actual lawn that is available to the employees to the nearest whole number?

(10) A student scores 45 marks in a standardized test. After some weeks of additional tuition his scores improve by 30%. What marks does he now get in a similar test?

(11) What is 12.5% of 360 Kilograms?

(12) A company has 950 employees. They encourage employees to join a variety of fitness classes. 15% join a gym class, 32% join a yoga class, 11% join a jogging group and the rest do not join any group. How many employees do not join any fitness class?

(13) A walking trip was organized. The map showed a scale of 1:100000. The main organizer planned out the route as follows:

Start from A and going to B total distance on the map =2.7cm

From B to C the distance on the map was 3.2 cm

Finally the distance from C to D was 8.2 cm

What was the distance in Kilometres from A to D?

(14) The head of Marketing orders some books and DVD's for some new employees in a particular department for some training. He orders are for 92 set books at £1.65 each, 220 Notebooks which come in packs of 10 at £4.60 per pack, and 8 Basic Training DVD's at £5.75 each. There is a Company discount of 12% on the total order. Calculate the total amount the order cost after the discount. Give your answer correct to 2 decimal places.

Question 15

In a year 11 group, there are 54 pupils altogether of which 24 are girls. Music lessons are taken by $\frac{1}{5}$ of the boys and $\frac{1}{4}$ of the girls. What is the total number of pupils from the year 11 group that take music lessons?

Answers to Practice Questions 2

(1) £65.20

Method: Each way is 81.5 miles. So there are 163 miles which includes the return journey @ 40p per mile

= 163 X 40p = £163 X 0.4 = £65.20

(2) 54

Method: There are 48 pupils altogether. 1 adult per 8 pupils means 6 adults are needed. (Since 48 ÷ 8 =6). This means there are a total of 48 + 6 people = 54 people on this trip.

(3) £1,320

Method: 1% of £22,000,000 (£22M) = £220,000

This means ½% = £110,000. Hence 1% + ½ % = £330,000

Since there are 250 front line staff, each member of the front line staff gets 330,000÷250 = 33000÷25 = 6600 ÷ 5 = £1,320

(4) £210,899 to the nearest pound

Method: From the beginning of 2005 to the end of 2012 consists of 8 years. If the price rises by 2% per annum for 8 consecutive years, then the price after 8 years is $180,000 \times (1.02)^8$. (Note that 1.02^8 means $1.02 \times 1.02 \times 1.02$..... up to 8 times) Hence £180,000 $\times 1.02^8$ = 210898.69 = £210,899 to the nearest pound.

(5) 13:35

Method: The presentation lasts 30 minutes and the Q&A session lasts 20 minutes. Hence the time taken for the meeting is 50 minutes. Since it ends at 14:25 we need to subtract 50 minutes from this to give us 13:35

(6) 420

Method: The ratio of male to female employees of 4:5 implies there are 9 parts in total. Since there are 945 employees in total, each part is equivalent to 105 employees. This means there are 420 male employees.

(7) £296.80

Method: Profit per book is £6.70 − 2.99 or we can say £6.71- £3 = £3.71. The profit for 10 books is £37.10, hence the profit for 80 books = £37.10 X 8 = £296.80

(Or else use a calculator)

(8) £1,615

Method: Total collected = £340 X 4.75 = £340X4 + £340X0.5 + £340X0.25 = £1360 + £170 + £85 = £1,615

(9) 35 m^2

Method: Lawn area available = area of rectangle − area of circular pond. Hence, lawn area available = 8.5X4.5 - πr^2 = 38.25 − 3.14X1X1 =38.25 − 3.14 = 35.11m^2 = 35m^2 to the nearest whole number

(10) 58.5 marks

Method: 30% of 45 = 45X0.3 = 13.5

We now need to add 13.5 to 45 to give us a total of 58.5 marks

(11) 45 kgm

Method: 12.5% = 10% + 2.5%

10% of 360 Kgm = 36, 5% =18 and 2.5% =9. So 10% +2.5% = 36 + 9 = 45kgm

(12) 399 employees

Method: Total percentage that join some fitness group = 15% + 32% + 11% = 58%. Hence 42% do not join any fitness group. 42% of 950 = 950X0.42 = 399

(13) 14.1 km

Method: Total distance on the map = 2.7 + 3.2 + 8.2 = 14.1 cm. Using a scale 1:100000. This means 14.1cm =14.1X100000cm =1410000cm = 14100 metres (divide1410000 by 100 to give the answer in metres). Finally, 14100 ÷1000 = 14.1 km

(14) £263.12

Method: Using a calculator

92 set books @ £1.65 each = £151.80, 220 notebooks in packs of 10 means 22 packs @ £4.60 each = £101.20, 8 training DVD's @ £5.75 each = £46. Total cost before discount = £151.80 + £101.20 + £46 = £299. Discount of 12% on £299 means the department pays £35.88 less

Hence actual amount paid for the order = £299 - £35.88 = £263.12

(15) 12 pupils

Method: There are 54 pupils altogether. 24 are girls, so 30 must be boys. Hence the number of pupils who take music lessons are:
$\frac{1}{4}$ of 24 plus $\frac{1}{5}$ of 30 = 6 + 6 = 12 pupils.

Practice Questions 3: Data interpretation with Multiple Choice

Calculators allowed

Question 1

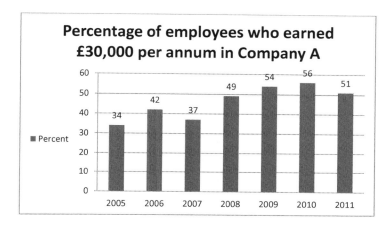

Percentage of employees who earned £30,000 per annum in Company A

(1) The mean percentage who earned £30,000 from 2008 to 2011 was:

    (a) 20%   (b) 21%   (c) 37%   (d) 52.5%   (e) 24.5%

(2) What was the percentage increase in employees that earned £30,000 from 2005 to 2011?

    (a) 26%   (b) 28%   (c) 17%   (d) 40%   (e)50%

Question 2

A teacher wanted to compare the progress of 8 pupils across two tests and see who had increased by at least 10 percentage points. The first test was out of 40 and the second test was out of 50. Which pupils meet this target?

Pupils	Test1 (marks out of 40)	Test 2 (marks out of 50)
A	22	32
B	25	32
C	17	27
D	25	35
E	19	26
F	12	20
G	25	34
H	30	47

(a) C, F & G   (b) C, E & G   (c) C, F & H   (d) A, C & D

(e) A, B & G

Question 3

Report: <u>The number of emergency admissions at 4 Hospitals on three days in the UK</u>

Hospital	Friday	Saturday	Sunday
Hospital A	200	210	90
Hospital B	180	160	100
Hospital C	250	150	60
Hospital D	150	120	20

(1) Which hospital had the most admissions for all three days combined?

(a) Hospital B   (b) Hospital A   (c) Hospital D   (d) Hospital C

(2) What is the percentage of admissions in Hospital A on a Sunday compared to all Hospitals on the same day?

(a) 31.33%   (b) 29.33%   (c) 33.33%   (d) 40%   (e) 72%

Question 4

Report: <u>E-Reader Sales in millions for March 2011</u>

<u>Country</u>	<u>Kindle</u>	<u>Ipad</u>	<u>Nook</u>
USA	2	1.5	0.02
UK	0.5	0.3	0.01
Germany	0.4	0.35	0.02
France	0.35	0.45	0.03

(1) How many Nook e-readers in thousands were sold in Europe during this month?
   (a) 8000   (b) 80,000   (c) 81,000   (d) 810,000 (e) 60000

(2) Which country had the least Kindle and Ipad sales combined?

   (a) USA   (b) UK   (c) Germany   (d) France

Question 5

<u>Annual sales report for 4 medium sized companies in 2010</u>

<u>Company</u>	<u>Annual Sales</u>	<u>Number of employees</u>
A	£4 million	50
B	£6 million	100
C	£2.4 million	60
D	£8 million	160

(1) Which company had the highest sales per employee?

 (a) Company A (b) Company B (c) Company C (d) Company D

(2) Company D had a 25% increase in sales in 2011. Also the number of employees increased by 40. What was the sales per employee in Company D in 2011?

 (a) £120,000   (b) £100,000   (c) £110,000 (d) £50,000   (e) £121,000

Question 6

The graph below shows the percentage of pupils achieving Grade C in Maths from 2006 to 2011.

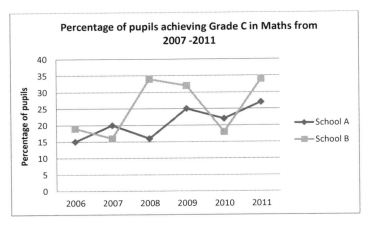

(1) By how many percentage points approximately did School B outperform School A in 2011?

(a) 17% (b) 7% (c) 10% (d) 15% (e) 12%

(2) What was the percentage point increase in achieving Grade C Maths in School A from 2006 to 2009?

(a) 15% (b) 10% (c) 20% (d) 5% (e) 25%

Question 7

The Deputy Head created the following table showing the number of pupils in each year group who had music lessons.

What is the percentage of pupils in all the year groups combined that have music lessons? Give your answer rounded to a whole number.

Year Group	Number of pupils	Number of pupils who have music lessons
7	92	10
8	101	18
9	105	14
10	96	13
11	102	11

(a) 21% (b) 13% (c) 19% (d) 20% (e) 22%

Question 8

The table below shows the total sales by a fashion retailer in London, Paris and New York

Total Sales	2008	2009	2010	2011
London shops (In Millions of £)	10.5	9.8	9.5	10.1
Paris shops (In Millions of Euros)	7.7	7.8	6.9	8.2
New York shops (In Millions of $)	15.1	14.3	14.6	14.9

(1) Assuming that in 2011 on average the exchange rates was £1 = 1.25 Euros and £1 = 1.6 US $. What were the total sales in 2011 for all three cities in pounds sterling. Give your answer in pounds million to two decimal places.

(a) £24.92M (b) £25.81M (c) £28.82M (d) £25.97M (e) £27.25M

(2) What was the percentage increase in Sales in Paris from 2008 to 2009, giving your answer correct to 1 decimal place?

(a) 1.2% (b) 4.1% (c) 2.1% (d) 1.3% (e) 2.2%

Question 9

An assistant meteorologist wants to convert a temperature of 22 degrees Celsius into Fahrenheit

The formula for converting the temperature from Celsius to Fahrenheit is given by:

$F= \dfrac{9}{5}C +32$ (where C is the temperature in degrees Celsius). If the temperature is 22 degrees Celsius what is the equivalent temperature in Fahrenheit?

(a) 70.2 degrees Fahrenheit (b) 71.6 degrees Fahrenheit (c) 81.6 degrees Fahrenheit (d) 71.5 degrees Fahrenheit   (e) 73.3 degrees Fahrenheit

Question 10

Two managers and 12 employees go to France on a team building session. The exchange rate at the time they go is £1 = 1.3 euros. The employees change £50 each and the managers £100 each for themselves before going to France. When they come back the exchange rate is £1 = 1.25 euros. If they convert all their Euros left back to pounds they get back £28. How much in Euros did they spend altogether whilst in France?

(a) 102.5 euros (b) 1025 euros (c) 1025.6 euros (d) 1003.6 euros (e) 1005 euros

Question 11

The set of data below shows the result in a year 10 Geography test for 96 pupils. The marks are out of 10. The teacher wants to find the mean mark for this test. Give your answer to 1 decimal place.

Marks in Geography Test	No of pupils	No. of pupils X Geography marks	
1	1	1 X 1 = 1	
2	5	2 X 5 = 10	
3	12		
4	22		
5	27		
6	18		
7	7		
8	3		
9	1		
10	0		
Totals	96		

The mean mark is:

(a) 5.1 (b) 4.9 (c) 4.8 (d) 6.2 (e) 12.1

Question 12

In one school 140 pupils took maths GCSE exams. Both the percentage of pupils as well as the GCSE Grades obtained in maths is shown in the pie chart below.

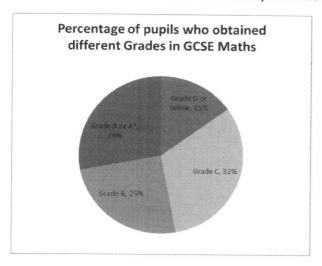

Percentage of pupils who obtained different Grades in GCSE Maths

- Grade D or below, 15%
- Grade A or A*, 28%
- Grade C, 32%
- Grade B, 25%

(1) What was the number of pupils who got Grade B?

   (a) 36   (b) 32   (c) 40   (d) 35   (e) 27

(2) The percentage of pupils who got Grade C or above was:

   (a) 86%   (b) 85%   (c) 87%   (d) 25%   (e) 92%

Question 13

The pie chart below shows the number of pupils who got a Grade C or better in English in four different schools

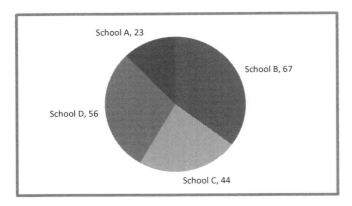

(1) The percentage of pupils who got Grade C or better in School C compared to all the other schools was approximately:

(a) 23.2%   (b) 24.5%   (c) 20.3%   (d) 21.2%   (e) 44.1%

(2) For grade C or better, the fraction of the total corresponding to School D was:

(a) $\frac{27}{95}$ (b) $\frac{28}{95}$ (c) $\frac{56}{95}$ (d) $\frac{28}{190}$ (e) $\frac{27}{190}$

Question 14

A teacher tells pupils that there will be a test in 4 weeks' time. She asks them to record their revision time over this period. Finally she shows the pupils the results of the maths test in relation to the time they spent revising in a scatter graph.

Scatter graph below shows the revision time in hours and resulting Maths marks

The number of pupils who get 50 marks or more in the test is:

(a) 7   (b) 6   (c) 8   (d) 3   (e) 9

Answers to Practice Questions 4

Question 1

(1) Answer (d) 52.5%

Method: The mean % of those that earned £30,000 from 2008 to 2011 = (49 + 54 + 56 + 51)/4 = 210÷4 =52.5%

(2) Answer: (e) 50%

Method: Increase in percentage points from 2005 to 2011 = 17%

This increase of 17% was from 34%. To find the percentage increase we calculate $\frac{17}{34}$ X100 = $\frac{1}{2}$ X 100 = 50% (Notice you can simplify $\frac{17}{34}$ to be equal to $\frac{1}{2}$ (cancel top and bottom by 17)

Question 2

Answer: (c) i.e. C, F & H

Method: Convert Test1 and Test2 into percentages first.

Hence in Test 1 and Test 2 the respective percentage marks for the pupils were:

Pupil A: 55% and 64%

Pupil B: 62.5% and 64%

Pupil C: 42.5% and 54%

Pupil D: 62.5% and 70%

Pupil E: 47.5% and 52%

Pupil F: 30% and 40%

Pupil G: 62.5% and 68%

Pupil H: 75% and 94%

So the pupils who had increased their marks by at least 10% from Test1 to Test2 were C, F and H

Question 3

(1) Answer (b) Hospital A

Method: The total admissions for the three days at the 4 hospitals were as follows: A =500, B = 440, C = 460, D = 290. Hence hospital A had the most admissions

(2) Answer (c) 33.33%

Method: Total admission on Sunday by the four hospitals = 90 + 100 +60 +20 =270. So percentage for Hospital A is $\frac{90}{270}$ x100 = $\frac{1}{3}$ x 100 =33.33%

Question 4

(1) Answer (e) 60,000

Method: The number of Nook E-readers sold in Europe (UK, Germany & France) for March 2011 = (0.01 + 0.02 +0.03) million

= 0.06 million = 0.06 X 1000000 = 60,000

(2) Answer (c) Germany

Method: Combined Kindle & Ipad sales by country is USA = 3.5M, UK = 0.8m, Germany = 0.75M, France = 0.8m. Hence, the least sales were in Germany.

Question 5

(1) Answer (a) Company A

Method: To work out sales per employee in each country divide sales (£m) by number of employees:

Company A = £80,000; Company B =£ 60,000; Company C= £40,000 and Company D= £50,000. Hence Company A has the highest sales'

(2) Answer (d) £50,000

Method: 25% increase from £8m means the new sales are now £10M. Also the employees increased by 40, so the new number of employees are now 200. Finally dividing £10m by 200 we get £50,000

Question 6

(1) Answer (b) 7% (approximately)

Method: From the line graph in 2011, school A achieved approx. 27% success in achieving Grade C in Maths.

Similarly, school B achieved 34%. Hence the difference was 7%

(2) Answer (b) 10%

Method: From the line graph the percentage of pupils achieving the GCSE grade C success changed from 15% in 2006 to 25% in 2009. Hence this amounted to an increase in 10 percentage points.

Question (7)

Answer (b) 13%

Method: Total number of pupils = 496. Total number of pupils who have music lessons = 66. Hence percentage of pupils who have music lesson =$\frac{66}{496}$X 100 = approx. 13%

Question (8)

(1) Answer (d) £25.97M

Method: Sales in £ sterling in 2011 were as follows:

London: £10.1M

Paris = 8.2 Million Euros, convert to sterling, 8.2÷1.25 = £6.56M

New York = 14.9 Million dollars, convert to sterling 14.9÷1.6 =£9.3125M. Adding up London, Paris & New York we get

10.1 + 6.56 + 9.3125 = £25.97M (to two decimal places)

(2) Answer (d) 1.3%

Method: increase in sales in Paris from 2008 to 2009 = 7.8 -7.7 = 0.1 million euros. Hence the percentage increase was $\frac{0.1}{7.7}$ x 100 = 1.3%

(1.3% is the answer to one decimal place)

Question 9

Answer (b) 71.6 degrees Fahrenheit

Method: Using the formula F= $\frac{9}{5}$ C +32 and substituting 22 degrees for C we get F = $\frac{9}{5}$ X 22 +32 = 39.6 +32 = 71.6 degrees Fahrenheit

Question 10

Answer (e) 1005 Euros

Method: Total euros obtained initially by 2 managers = (£100X2X1.3) = 260

Total euros obtained by 12 employees= £50X12X1.3 = 780 euros

Grand total = 260 +780 = 1040 euros. However if they convert all their euros into pounds they get back £28. So at the given exchange rate (1.25 euros = £1), they must have had 1.25X28 euros left = 35 euros. Hence they must have spent (1040 – 35) euros altogether. That is 1005 Euros.

Question 11

Answer (b) 4.8

Method: Fill in the table as shown first:

Marks in Geography Test	No of pupils	No. of pupils X Geography marks	
1	1	1 X 1 = 1	
2	5	2 X 5 = 10	
3	12	3X12 =36	
4	22	4X22 =88	
5	27	5X27 = 135	
6	18	6X18 = 108	
7	7	7X7 =49	
8	3	8X3 =24	
9	1	9X1 =9	
10	0	10X0 =0	
Totals	96	460	

Now divide 468 by 96 to get the mean value. 460÷96 = 4.79166 or 4.8 to 1 decimal place.

Question 12

(1) Answer (d) 35

Method: From the pie chart you can see that 25% got a grade B. Since there are 140 pupils altogether, this means 25% of 140 = 25. (50% of 140 =70, so 25% of 140 = 35)

(2) Answer (b) 85%

Method: From the pie chart it can be seen that 32% got a grade C, 25% got a grade B and 28% got grade A or A*. Hence the total percentage who got a grade C or above is 32% + 25% + 28% = 85%

Question 13

(1) Answer (a) 23.2%

Method: From the pie chart the total number of pupils who got a grade C or better in English in the four schools were: 23(School A) + 67(School B) + 44(School C) + 56(School D) = 190 pupils. In school C the percentage was: $\frac{44}{190}$X 100 = 23.2% (to 1 decimal place)

(2) Answer (b) $\frac{28}{95}$

Method: Total number of pupils who made grade C or better in School D = 56. Hence the corresponding fraction compared to all schools is $\frac{56}{190}$, this simplifies to $\frac{28}{95}$

Question (14)

Answer: (b) 6

Method: From the scatter graph draw an imaginary horizontal line at 50 marks. The number of (points) pupils above this line corresponds to 6.

Made in the USA
Coppell, TX
05 August 2021